RF ||||||||||||||||||||||||||||||

Don't Let Sand Fool You

So many people today are under the deceptive impression that God only impacts their world for "the big stuff". The danger of this is believing He isn't involved or doesn't want to be bothered with the routine, mundane, smaller irritants we encounter. *Don't Let Sand Fool You* debunks this ideology right from the start. The author embeds this truth on every page: Irritants are never wasted when we allow God to use them on our behalf.

Ingrid Simmonds' phrase, "from grains to grit and into a pearl" captures our imagination and gives the reader an immediate realization that this will not be an ordinary book proclaiming a few life-defining victories. Ingrid has thoughtfully laid out her authentic journey with sobering transparency, encountering grains of all sizes, more grit than she ever thought she had and deliberate encouragement for all of us thriving or surviving on our path to becoming Pearls!

— **Joni Hennigan Lora,** Senior Business Development Manager, 9-Year Cancer Thriver.

***

Ingrid has captured the very essence of Transformation. Her inspirational story reveals the joy of being transported from adversity to victory; what it looks like to be delivered from tremendous physical, spiritual, and emotional attacks through an intimate relationship with Jesus Christ. Having survived a debilitating illness myself, I applaud and admire her strength, courage, and steadfast faith. This story could have been written from the perspective of a two-time victim

i

of cancer -for she was exactly that-, but it was not. I don't believe Ingrid ever saw herself as a victim. She epitomizes what it means to be a *conqueror through Christ.*

—**Sue Arrington,** Christian Speaker and Author of *Killin' Snakes.*

***

This book is a manifestation of a heart for God. If you thought you could not still be used by God in this season, this is a guide to turning your test into a testimony and your mess into your message. It is a practical guide to learning how to count your days because they are numbered by the Lord. The lessons on how we find God's voice in the unpleasantness of our human existence is inspirational and challenging. "God is faithful to use you as you are". It's hard to comprehend when all you see are the scars of your life, but those scars are your unique stamp and you can rest in the fact that " God created you to be you". After reading this, I am refreshed, revived, and redirected to be a thriver, not a survivor. Thank you for sharing this journey. I no longer feel alone.

— **Floyd Smith,** Retired Associate Pastor of *Calvary Chapel Los Alamos*, Husband to Loretta Smith for 50 years, cancer thriver.

***

If you have ever been hit hard with difficulty and wondered how in the world to navigate through it, read this book. If you haven't, read it to learn more about how to walk through life's inevitable future trials, and come out the other side with the beauty and strength of a forged character. The author's revelation of her intimate relationship with God, distilled over a lifetime, yields wisdom and rich fruit for the reader to pick and savor.

— **Jaqueline Weaver**.

Being the Almighty God of our past, present, and future, God always has His ways of accomplishing His purposes set before us. God already knows the paths that we will walk, and the people that will be there to join us by His purpose. God gave Ingrid a passion to write. God has used that passion to share her story and His testimony in her of His faithfulness.

God introduced Ingrid and I in college and allowed us to wander apart, but walk purposefully with Him in other parts of the world (some wildernesses) for **40** years. Now, God is bringing us and others in the world together to urge us to know our story and His testimony in each of us. Through "Don't Let Sand Fool You, Sand to Pearl Transformation", God is meeting me in my brokenness regarding my husband's recent death and the realization of the sudden strong internal need to seek Him and His ways in my healing. My conviction of legacy and His testimony is affirmed through Ingrid's learning family stories and her story, and sharing with her children and grandchildren (Joshua 4). God is in the process of transforming me, grain by grain, through the sand of grief. I will think differently each time I stick my feet in the sand. I could be stepping on the next pearl.

— **Dee Ann Gibbs**, Disciple of Christ, Bible Study Facilitator, and retired Special Education Teacher.

DON'T LET SAND FOOL YOU

INGRID SIMMONDS

References

Noah Webster's First Edition of an American Dictionary of the English Language (1st Ed.) (2004). Foundation for American Christian Education. Chesapeake, VA.

Unless otherwise indicated, all Scripture quotations are taken from the Holy Bible, New International Translation, Life Application Study Bible. (2005/1988). Used by permission of Zondervan and Tyndale House Publishers, Wheaton, IL.

Unless otherwise indicated, all Scripture quotations are taken from the Holy Bible, New Living Translation. (2015/1996). Used by permission of Tyndale House Publishers, a Division of Tyndale House Ministries, Carol Stream, Illinois 60188. All rights reserved.

Unless otherwise indicated, all Scripture quotations are taken from THE MESSAGE. (2018/1993). Eugene H. Peterson. Used by permission of NavPress. Represented by Tyndale House Publishers, a Division of Tyndale House Ministries. All rights reserved.

TABLE OF CONTENTS

Acknowledgement

Thank you to my loving, attentive, supportive, servant-heart husband Stanley, who took such awesome care of me.

To my sons, Isaac and Matthew and their wives, Krystal and Abby, who encouraged and motivated me to fight to live.

Thank you especially to my daughter Rachel, for all the housework she did and for hanging out with me. She was the best chef, even though all I ate for months were mashed potatoes and peanut butter milkshakes.

Thank you to Floyd, my Pastor, friend, and encourager, for encouraging me to write, for asking me tough questions about my walk, but requiring me to come up with the answers.

Chapter 1

Revelations in an Ocean Full of Sand

In this godless world you will continue to experience difficulties. But take heart! I've conquered the world. John 16:33 (The Message)

So be strong and courageous. Do not panic before them, for the Lord your God will personally go ahead of you; He will never fail you nor abandon you. Deut. 31:6 (New International Version)

...When troubles of any kind come your way, consider it an opportunity for great joy. For you know that when your faith is tested, your endurance has a chance to grow. So let it grow, for when your endurance is fully developed, you will be perfect and complete, needing nothing." James 1:2-4 (NIV)

November of 2005, I was doing my usual morning routine. I was showering when I felt a hard lump about the size of a marble in my breast. I was scheduled for a mammogram in a few weeks, but for my peace of mind, I nervously called and asked to come in that day. The doctor felt around a bit and then said, "Let's go downstairs for a mammogram". The doctor then walked me downstairs and put me ahead of the scheduled patients. In my mind, I was thinking, *this is not a good sign. When does a doctor ever personally escort you to another doctor?* The radiology team did an ultrasound and one of the radiologists told me I had cancer and showed me the image. I was stunned. As far as I was concerned, nobody in my family or my husband's family had ever had cancer.

When I saw my gynecologist, she asked to take me to the surgeon's office and get a biopsy done right away to confirm our suspicions. Immediately we got there, they took me right back to the lab, and they did a biopsy. Throughout the day, I had left my kids at home (they were high school age) and my husband was out of town. When my 15-minute appointment took three hours, I knew my kids would begin to wonder what was up.

Everything happened so FAST! I went home feeling like a zombie and didn't even know what to think or do. I was stunned and overwhelmed. Telling my husband when he got home was even harder. Who wants to come home to that kind of news? After we talked, I had a good cry.

The phone rang and it was the nursing home where my father lived; they were telling me my father probably wouldn't live through the night. Still overwhelmed by my own news that day, I went with my mother to the home and spent time with him. It took my focus off my cancer for a short time till he passed away that night.

On Monday morning, I had an appointment with the surgeon for my biopsy results, and thus, went in the company of my husband. Dealing with my father's death had not given me much time to worry about my biopsy report. By that morning, my heart was racing in anticipation of what the doctor would say. He said he didn't have good news and confirmed later that it was cancer. I burst into tears and lost my composure. The doctor tried to calm me down, assuring me it was good news that the tumor was small had been discovered early. My husband explained to him that my father had passed away that weekend. The doctor excused himself and quickly left the room. Eventually, he came back and apologized for the timing of his news and my loss.

We buried my dad the next day and I had surgery the following Monday. I didn't have much time to think about my health and just did as the doctor suggested. I barely had time to mourn my Dad before I began to fight for my survival. My life had become a hurricane of one storm after another, rolling, overwhelming me, and stretching my faith. The bright spot in this was that the cancer was only Stage 1 and had not spread to my lymph nodes. Notwithstanding this, my treatment would be chemotherapy and radiation.

My comfortable life was shattered with one jaw-dropping circumstance after another. Months later, after grieving and accepting my diagnosis, my thoughts left me confused as to what my purpose was. There must be more to life. I would tell my children jokingly, "Life is hard and then you die." But was I joking?

I began to wonder and realized I needed to change the way I viewed life. My attitude was not one of living life to the fullest with God by my side. I wasn't claiming all the declarations and promises the Lord had shown us about ourselves in His Word. Yes, I had been a Christian for a long time; I felt my walk was "fine." Yes, life was hard but there's more to it. We must choose to make the best of it, be all we can be, and cling to His promises to guide us through.

During my childhood years, there were fairly gentle storms, but they were ones I knew I could not handle on my own. To me at present, I faced rain-soaking, thunderous, ominous storms. They were life-changing. I needed someone greater than myself to intervene and walk with me. I chose to stay as close to God as I could. In my mind, what other choice did I have?

Before my father passed away, waves of trials were already wearing me down. I had already spiraled into a world of close family members who desperately needed my care and attention. And though my father's death was not a surprise, it was challenging. Before my cancer diagnosis, I had already begun feeling like I had several one-sided relationships where I did all the work and was exhausted. I felt like nobody was taking care of me, so I went into my health fight already exhausted in every way and mentally overwhelmed.

The doctors had never formulated a diagnosis for my father, but his brain was disintegrating. His care took countless hours and boundless energy. He was slowly losing his quality of life and more's the pity. He was aware of it too. At the same time, I was struggling to be a support for my mother who was so tired and overwhelmed with his care and so many medical appointments a hundred miles away and struggling to home-school my high school daughter. All of this was happening at the time of my cancer diagnosis. Shock upon shock took a toll upon my strength, emotions, and mind. Yes, all this had a purpose, but not the one I wanted. I was told God has a purpose for everyone. I was not convinced, yet. Unaware of it at the time, I would soon learn to find my purpose in life and find my value.

Unless and until we learn a life lesson from each circumstance or event we go through, it will be for nothing. Having been diagnosed with breast cancer, I felt I had been given a second chance at life and was choosing to make the best of what I had left, and not let it all be a waste. I wanted to change for the better and also needed to try and help at least one person learn from my journey. I CHOSE to be positive, to focus on God, and not to be defeated.

After the funeral, my surgery, and Christmas, I began chemo and radiology treatments. Life became busier and busier, despite my dwindling-to-disappearing strength. I lacked the energy to be there for my mother who did not even have a chance or enough time to mourn my father's death before she began fighting for me. Living with joy or enthusiasm slid to the back burner for us, and I pushed God away. I lost my purpose for living. I had no stamina or motivation for family, church relationships, or friendships, all of which need people working from both ends-. I was tired and unmotivated to read the Word or talk to God. My desire to be upbeat and positive while fighting this battle soon dwindled to frustration and discouragement.

Not only had I no motivation to fight, but also, I questioned why I had to fight at all. I thought, *Why fight when I have no comprehension of my worth or if I have any place in His heart?* I had no idea I was still useful. My light was dimming to just a small, glowing circle, yet I reminded myself I wanted to leave a bright legacy to my children and future grandchildren. With that bit of motivation, even amidst the battle I faced, I began the search for answers to these deep heart and soul questions. I knew it only took a bit of motivation the size of a mustard seed to plant and grow into a fruitful, satisfying, God-blessed life.

It was a simple beginning so I started with one thing: reading the Word each day and listening. One by one, God began giving me words of hope and encouragement. I began writing pages and pages of what I was learning. I started writing to use as my therapeutic journal (maybe I would attempt to get published one day). At one point, though, I decided this was silly. Where did I ever get the idea that I had any wisdom to share with anybody else? I put my writing away, but little "coincidences" would pop up periodically, reminding me of my writing. One of such was when a nurse before an unrelated surgery asked what I did for fun. I told her I enjoyed writing but had dropped it for a while. As we got talking, she encouraged me to continue writing; so, it turned out that "pearl" encouraged me to keep on going.

You're reading this book, so it is obvious that when I face another battle or victory and feel the urge to put it on paper, I will pull out my pen and begin writing again.

At times, God was so quiet that I was disheartened and feared He had moved away from me. The truth, however, is that God never moves away from us; we are the ones who move away from Him. Regardless of whether God was there or not, I considered His silence as His not being there or caring. I felt that His silence meant He was not going to intervene in my life. Of course, He was not necessarily silent either; I simply did not hear what I wanted to hear. God was not the one who moved further away; I was. I was the one who did not recognize His voice, was the one who pulled away. As I contemplated what friends I could call, no name came to mind. I also didn't feel it was my place to call upon people in my time of need when I had not been there for them in their needs. It was important to me to know God was there and I desired a friend; someone to be there in my life, in the highs and lows, ups and downs, and the exciting or the boring.

My deep desire was simply to live life to the fullest and that had to begin when I changed my attitude and began to seek Him with all my heart. It was also about finding my worth in my existence and knowing I was able to fight battles with His help. It was about finding meaningful purpose in my life. I chose to seek God first. Once I was on my path, then I would find my purpose and my worth. I wasn't going to just pass through and wander around. I was going to use His Word as my guide. When rocks and holes would be scattered on my path, I wanted to learn how to navigate through them or around them and continue towards His purpose for my life.

Learning to accept a cancer diagnosis was a struggle for me. As I said, nobody in my immediate or near-immediate family had ever been diagnosed with cancer. I was only 44 and still had two of my three children at home. Where did the cancer come from? As I tried to know more about cancer, I also tried *to learn more about God in this part of my journey.*

The night before my surgery, I was frantically pacing my bedroom, totally frustrated and stressed about my situation. I picked up my Bible from the nightstand and flung it across the floor; it landed open at Isaiah 43:1-12. A square of moonlight shone through the window, illuminating only those verses in Isaiah 43. I read them and let them soak in. I clung to Isaiah 43:1-

4, believing the Holy Spirit impressed upon me that I would not die from this cancer. I would live long. I would live to see and meet all my future grandchildren and be a spiritual mentor to them; and though none of my children was married at that time, that was the interpretation I felt was strongly impressed upon me. So, here I was, pulling away from Him, yet He was there to speak a word to my heart *when* I needed it most. We must never mistake God's silence for His lack of love and care for us. Could it be possible we have plugged our spiritual ears?

After surgery and treatment, life went back to normal. In early 2009, three years after my father passed away, my mother passed followed after losing her battle to kidney cancer. She never recovered from the death of my father, and just like myself, she had been stressed out and barely fought to live. During her fight with kidney cancer, I continuously spent time caring for her. Don't get me wrong, I am not complaining about caring for my parents. I treasure the time spent taking care of everyone, and despite it being tiring and emotionally draining, I wanted to take care of them and spend as much time as I could with them because of the love I had for them; And I did this without regret.

In April 2010, my daughter (the last child left at home) moved away, leaving my husband and me with an empty nest. I had heard horror stories about "empty nest syndrome", and I kind of dreaded it, but that was not much of a problem for me. My problem was missing family members who had departed permanently, and not just moved across the country. My closest family members had moved on with their lives. My husband worked all day every day and often traveled. I went from the last four years of constantly being needed, being busy, being mentally and emotionally overwhelmed, to absolutely NOTHING! My crazy, busy, hectic, time-consuming days dropped to nothing. I plugged my ears as I spent my days focusing on myself and lamenting the negatives over and over in mind.

I thought about life -mostly the negative-, after everyone had moved on, and more and more, I felt like it was me they left. I took it personally. Everything and everybody was out to make my life more difficult. The truth was, nobody left me. They moved forward with God's call in their lives or to be with Our Heavenly Father. Their absence did not make me grow fonder of them or God, but again, it caused me to search deep within myself and His Word.

I wondered, *What's next for me? What now? What do I do or not do? What is my purpose? What good can come from this? Where are my friends?* My life seemed meaningless and compared to three years ago, I seemed to have no more purpose now. Most importantly, I was still a wife but I no longer had the duties of mother, daughter, or caretaker. I didn't even make a valid attempt to fill the hole in my life as day after day, I was occupied with tears. My husband would come home from work and find me on the couch, crying my eyes out. The despair and emotional pain made it worse. I knew my thoughts had to change. I had to find a new purpose. I had to do *something*! Anything!

My walk with the Lord was lacking too; not because I doubted Him or lost faith, but because I craved purpose and relationships here on earth. I craved a depth with Him and just being in His presence. I wanted attention and direction. I wanted friends. I wanted someone who would listen to me to talk to. I wanted to know God still cared for me as a specific individual. My heart desired to know Him more, regardless of my circumstances.

Later that year, I decided I could use a job to keep my mind occupied, be physically out of the house, and be around other people. I thought that might be a start to the answer I sought. People were friendly and I enjoyed short conversations here and there. I established working relationships and that was a start, yet, deep within me, I felt something was missing. There was a deep longing to share my life and my cancer journey with someone besides my husband. I didn't want to share only my challenging cancer story, but also my joys with someone and encourage others. I wanted to know there was purpose in all the pain I had endured. I didn't want my difficult season to be wasted. I wanted to use it for Him. I knew when we feel empty, the cure is to help others.

I knew I must learn to seek Him, find my satisfaction in Him and not in other people. Yet, I continued to look for new people to be friends with. I think I had just one friend who would ask how I was doing expecting an honest answer. Not finding the kind of relationships I craved, I began pulling away from the church. I wasn't finding what I needed there. I realized later I was going about all this the wrong way. When you're alone, you cannot pull back further from people; you must step forward in faith and attempt to begin friendships or revive old ones. And, you need to know or remember that no person can meet any of your needs. God is the ONLY one who can meet you where you are and fill your needs. Seek Him first, and other relationships will fall into place with your willingness and help. For me, that was a place to start.

For Christmas, a few years after my battle with breast cancer, we decided our minds and bodies could use a rest- the kind that takes you away from everything-. We took a cruise to Hawaii and Tahiti, and one day, while having a conversation about buying pearls in Tahiti, out of the blue, I heard information about pearls that I never knew. I learned about the characteristics of pearls and could relate them to me and my life. Seemed an odd place and time, but I went with it and it continued throughout different talks on different gemstones. I began to listen more seriously. I didn't realize what an educational and life-changing the journey would become.

The first lesson came during the first talk on pearls. I heard, "You are a pearl." The voice said, "You are a pearl to Him." None of us can develop from sand into a pearl in an instant; it's a long, slow process. It's not about the pearl, but about the transformation process. Transformation requires patience, pacing yourself, resting at times, and God's direction. "The Master, Jesus Christ, who will transform our earthly bodies into glorious bodies like His own. He'll make us beautiful and whole with the same powerful skill by which He is putting everything as it should be. Under and around Him." (Phil. 3:20-21) [MSG]

In contrast to a pearl, He first chose me, then He allowed irritants and grains of sand into my life, then He would show me how to turn them from grains to grit and into a pearl. I had the choice to use each grain to help me change and grow or to just let that grain eat away at me. He showed me how to let Him transform me from spiritual death to life. He showed me how He could transform me from the inside-out if I would let Him. I would be set free from mere obligatory Christianity to a direction-driven passion that would be satisfying and fulfilling. I would have to be obedient and learn to listen to the Holy Spirit. I had to learn to be disciplined in prayer, reading His Word, and listening. I had to do my part and He would do His.

In the first month of the next year, God allowed me to see if I was learning what He had been teaching me. I was diagnosed with Stage 3c ovarian cancer, and it had spread quite a bit. *Whoa!! Where did that come from? Hadn't I just learned about trusting God in difficult situations?*

The truth and the facts were, I had cancer that was quickly spreading. It doesn't really sink in when you hear the words, "You have cancer." You don't get it at that moment. Later, as it sinks in, you begin to understand. After crying on and off for three days, I started searching the internet for a prognosis and became overwhelmingly fearful. I began to pray for guidance and help. I felt like the Holy Spirit was telling me not to look to man for my future or prognosis. So, I quit looking on the internet. Don't choose the doctor's report and words over God's Word.

I had to trust God, not others, and not focus on the information in front of me that looked impossible. I reminded myself that my days were numbered by Him anyway, so it didn't matter. Again, God used Isaiah 43 to help me navigate through this difficult mental, emotional and physical journey.

I have called this first part of my story *a journey* because a journey gets you from one place to another.

I am going from cancer to being well, but from this point on, this is my pilgrimage. It's not just going from one place to another; I am going to a place that is holy. I am going from the devastation in a life journey to a place of holiness. I will be sanctified. I am going from this earth to an eternal, holy mansion. "I am the Lord who brought you up out of Egypt to be your God; therefore, be holy, because I am holy." (Lev. 11:45) [NIV]

This is now my pilgrimage story, even though I have not yet arrived there. Along the way, God tied my pilgrimage in with pearls instead of stones.

In addition to learning about pearls, ovarian cancer was the beginning of a challenging and difficult spiritual transition for me. However, I never asked, "Why me?" My thought was, *Why not me? I am no different from anybody else. I have cancer as a result of living in a fallen world. God didn't make me sick, but He can still use my sickness.* We are all equally dependent on God for our next breath, with cancer, sickness, or complete health. I now had a purpose: Fight and live! It was not a purpose I would have chosen, but it was a purpose nonetheless. And, in the process, I found another purpose: to share my testimony with others. Over the next few years, I continued to learn about pearls. I learned I am His precious pearl; my relationship with Him and time were the keys to being transformed.

God's grace is the reason the nation of Israel is transforming from nothing into existence. Israel is God's creation, and no one can destroy it. (Isaiah 43:1) [NIV] I am God's creation, and no one can destroy me. God's grace is bringing me from nothing to something. Growing and slowly being transformed from nothing into His image are as important as the pearl or the fruit.

This pilgrimage is about winding in and out of storms and calm seas to becoming a pearl. I knew He would carry me to a place of immeasurable peace and safety, so long as I let Him command my storms and use them. Each grain of sand was an opportunity in my journey for me to make me who I am and to become more like Him.

Each day, a new layer was added to my pearl that I hoped would reflect Christ and His love to all who were looking for encouragement. My grains were anything from my worth, to His purpose for me, to transforming myself into His character and image. My faith was stretched and my listening ear for God's voice was turned up a notch. I now moved forward in Christ's strength. "This is a case of Christ's strength moving in on my weakness. Now I take limitations in stride, and with good cheer... I just let Christ take over! And so, the weaker I got, the stronger I become" (2 Cor. 12:9-10 MSG).

He chose us in the beginning because He LOVES us. All we need to do is choose Him and submit control of our lives to Him.

"Anchor yourself to Christ; refuse to be separated and sink!" Ingrid Simmonds

Chapter 2

Created in His Image

Who can find a virtuous and capable wife? She is more precious than rubies. **Prov. 31:10 [NIV]**

So, God created man in His own image, in the image of God He created them; male and female He created them. **Genesis 1:27 [NIV]**

The son is the image of the invisible God, the firstborn over all creation., **Col. 1:15 [NIV]**

In Genesis, God created the light and dark, day and night. He created the sun and the stars. He created sky, land, and water. He created animals on land, birds in the air, and fish in the seas. He created human beings, male and then female. He saw everything He created and pronounced it good.

How amazing and awesome it is, after looking at all that beauty, He decided to create each one of us. He created us into human form from dust. We will be transformed into His image. Just like a photograph, the image ought to glorify the original. We are created in His image to be able to glorify Him. When we are "born again," He begins transforming us even more deeply in His image. It is a slow, time-consuming transformation, but worth the time. Since we are made in the likeness of God, out of love for us, He continues to change us.

Who can find a virtuous woman? God can. And we are worth more than rubies to Him. Who are we in Christ? We are God's chosen people, even with our flaws. We are born physically and then we are given the opportunity to accept Him as Our Savior and be born again. After accepting Him, we begin to grow spiritually throughout our lives, and we are transformed to be like Him and bring Him glory.

We become beautiful pearls made in His image; that was the first bit of wisdom I learned from Him. We continue to grow, both through our calm seas and through the rough storms we experience. We grow in the ups and downs of life, and within relationships, so we become whom He needs us to be. That growing process produces purpose and transforms us to be more like Him.

We are virtuous. We develop much worth and become usable to Him. Webster's 1828 dictionary defines virtuous as "being in conformity to the moral law." A virtuous woman is excellent because of her high morals and values. She is more than a jewel. All our life experiences, challenging or smooth, are designed to transform us to be excellent, made in His image, usable and precious; all of us being transformed into strong pearls in the circle of life. We are each being transformed from a simple form to a radiant, virtuous pearl.

Did He create us to go through difficult, challenging experiences and seasons? Did He want our transformation to be difficult? Both are at least partly true because we live in a fallen world where challenges and difficulties happen. Other times, our transformation is difficult because that is the way Our Father gets our attention. Once He has our attention, He can show us love, strength and power as He works in our situation. If we allow them, challenges and struggles build Godly character in us, including thoughts, attitudes, experiences, and relationships.

God never promised He would remove us from tough human experiences when we accept Him. He did promise, however, to be with us in ALL things and to give us strength. "For I can do everything through Christ who gives me strength." (Phil 4:13) [NIV] Through that roller coaster ride, we come to know Him on a deeper level and become more like Him.

Years ago, I had a friend who gave birth prematurely to a baby girl. Somehow, the pregnancy hadn't gone as planned and the mother ended up in the ICU with blood clots in her lungs. It was a grave, scary situation. I feared she would not be with us much longer. I went to bed that night asking God, "Why?" Why must we go through life with such difficult circumstances at times? I knew the answer but questioned Him anyway.

The Lord gave me a dream that night. I dreamed my friend was a paper doll with pages of many outfits that were bright and colorful, and she had all kinds of accessories, flowers, hats, shoes, and jewelry. This paper doll smiled and was fun and cheery to look at. I saw a large hand come down and began erasing all the accessories and colors, one by one. It erased until nothing was left but the outline of a body and a simple dress. In this dream, I was yelling, "Stop!" but the hand continued with its vigorous erasing. With every outfit that was erased, the paper doll's smile lessened, until she had no emotion. A voice said, "Look what happens to the person who has no struggles or challenges. They are dull, simple and unchanging. There is no life and joy in them. But, as they overcome a trial, they get a cheery color or a pair of shoes or a ribbon in their hair. Every trial they conquer adds to their character, making them who they are. Adversity brings life to them. Every joyous occasion they celebrate adds character to them. Beautiful, intricately designed people don't just happen; they achieve their beauty by how they transform in their suffering and in their joyous times." My friend was acquiring a new level of beauty through her trial.

As we know, not all aspects of believers' transformations are easy. God could take away the difficulties, but He probably won't. Most adversities or life experiences will be difficult and will challenge us beyond what we think we can handle, but if everything were smooth and followed *our* plan, we would not have needed a Savior.

"Blessed is the man who remains steadfast under trial, for when he has stood the test, he will receive the crown of life which God has promised to those who love Him" (James 1:12 ESV). I realized, to change me into more of His image and into becoming a beautiful pearl, I would have to go through trials. My trials were and are changing me. God showed me that as I changed into a pearl, I gained more worth than a ruby, emerald, sapphire, diamond, or any other gem. Whether we are aware of it or not, we are valuable to other people, not just to Him. Our not knowing this, not believing it, nor acknowledging it, does not change the facts. I am still a transformation with great value. God makes all the difference in the world regarding who I am and who you are, but we are valuable wherever we are, spiritually, mentally, emotionally and/or physically.

He invites us to accept Him as we are. He loves us

where we are in our lives at any given time, and He moves forward in changing us because He loves us. He promises us not only a beautiful transformation but also the crown of life if we love Him and remain steadfast through trials. Blessings are on the other side!

After the Lord began showing me the characteristics of pearls, I wondered what the definition of a pearl was. Of course, I knew it was round and had a lustrous shell. More than that, what was it specifically? What were its characteristics? The dictionary's definition of "pearl" is: "one that is choice and very precious." We are very precious and choice to God. He chose me to be His treasure. He chose you. "For you are a people holy to the Lord your God. Out of all the peoples on the face of the earth, the Lord has chosen you to be His treasured possession" (Deut. 14:2NIV). He cherishes us because we are ALL His workmanship. He planned for each of us, even before we were born. He has created us and identifies us as His. As He changes us, He chooses to display His glory in us, if we let Him.

God is our oyster shell. He surrounds us and protects us. He determines what comes in and out of our lives. He is the one who chooses us and when we accept Him in return, we begin to understand who we are. He knows we need irritants and sand to move us forward into the slow process of becoming more like Him.

To understand the importance of who we are as individuals, and how we portray His image, I believe it is significant to understand who we are in Christ, so *whose* we are is vital to our pilgrimage to become more like Him. "For we are God's masterpiece. He has created us anew in Christ Jesus, so we can do the good things He planned for us long ago." (Eph. 2:10) [NIV]

He is our example of who we ought to be. He is our Creator and Transformer. We are His workmanship. The importance of how we were created by God and how we overcome challenging life circumstances is crucial.

(**Author's note:** *When I use the word "believer" throughout this book, it means you believe and have submitted total control of your life to God. Anybody can believe, but true believers submit control to Him.*)

As believers in Christ, our identity is in Him, neither in what other people believe or say about us nor what we wrongly think or say about ourselves.

Have you ever felt like people put on you labels that do not define you, and yet you find yourself living up to them? Or have others already labeled you in their minds, and do not give you a chance to be who you really are? It is hard work to peel off those labels. I have to remind myself I am not always other people's labels. Sometimes, those labels create a false identity for us. I know I am the sum of who God made me, plus my journey, plus how I respond to irritants and sand in my life.

I will respond to whatever grains are thrown at me. Even giving up and doing nothing is a response. "But you are the ones chosen by God, chosen for the high calling of priestly work, chosen to be a holy people, God's instruments to do His work and speak out for Him, to tell others of the night-and-day difference He made for you-from nothing into a precious person, from rejected to accepted." (1 Peter 2:9) [MSG]

We are chosen (called) and labeled as His holy people to do His work and for others to see His power in us. "You didn't choose me, remember; I chose you, and put you in the world to bear fruit, fruit that won't spoil" (John 15:16MSG). Start believing what God says about you and not what others say. Believe in God and yourself, and your transformation will come; fruit will follow. God's labels for us are loved, chosen, forgiven, redeemed, sons and daughters, disciples and so much more!

"Submit yourselves, then, to God. Resist the devil and he will flee from you" (James 4:7NIV). If you have voices -Satan's whispered lies- in your mind telling you who you are, that you are not enough, or something or someone doesn't line up with God's Word, ask God to remind you again and to show you who you are. The world's opinions and labels of you and your personality will never change God's plan or how He sees you. We were created to become like Him, to be transformed into His image. The more we seek Him and learn from Him, the more we become like Him.

In Him, as believers, we are labeled by God as loved, forgiven, precious, priceless, cherished one-of-a-kind pearls. Believe He has created us for a purpose and destiny (Isaiah 43:7NIV) Ask Him! He will show you.

If you are a believer, go straight to Him and His Word. The Word is our source for telling us who we are as individuals, and who we are as a part of the Body of Christ. Your name and value are written on every page of His Word. Write those words on your heart. Align yourself with God's Word. Allow the Holy Spirit's indwelling in you to transform and change your thoughts about yourself. The more you read His Word, the more you know Him and love Him. "His powerful Word is sharp as a surgeon's scalpel, cutting through everything... Nothing and no one is pervious to God's Word" (Heb. 4:12-13MSG).

Ephesians 2:10 says we are His workmanship. We are created and loved by Him. As we are forming a relationship with Him, we are changing from Christians who are just going through the motions, into believers who are accepting renewal, restoration, and change, so we may become more like Him. He created us so we each have our unique characteristics to be the person we are. Because of those characteristics, we each write a different life story, including our part in the Body of Christ. You will find your purpose and learn to fulfill it through your experiences, personality, attitudes, and whatever else makes you who you are. Nobody can be who I am. Nobody can be who you are.

Ephesians further states He also "prepared us beforehand." To "prepare a person beforehand" is to qualify us for a purpose before we are born. After He had prepared us, we came into being in this world. We are ready to be transformed into a different kind of new creation.

After we have "arrived," the struggle begins for us and thinking we are not usable, thinking we are replaceable, not important, and so on. He already pre-qualified us for a different and unique purpose greater than the enemy's lies about us. "The very things we would assume disqualify us from fulfilling God's call are often what qualify us for it. Our human weaknesses and natural limitations give God a perfect opportunity to make Himself strong in us."[1] He desires

---

[1] Morris, D. (2013) *The Blessed Woman*, Waterbrook Press. pg. 20

for us to grow up and to know we qualify for whatever He has called us to do.

So, who am I? I am chosen by Him, created in His image, and becoming more and more like Him in my everyday walk through a life of joys and heartaches. My goal is to be a photocopy of His actions, love, and character in the world and to the world. Every priceless pearl is layers and layers of learning, changing, and growing to transform into being more like Him. "We are already God's children, but He has not yet shown us what we will be like when Christ appears. But we do know that we will be like Him, for we will see Him as He really is" (I John 3:20 NLT)

"The sea is His and He made it." Psalm 95:5 (KJV)

Chapter 3

Simple Form to Pearl Transformation

And so, we are transfigured much like the Messiah, our lives gradually becoming brighter and more beautiful as God enters our lives and we become like Him. **2 Cor. 3:18 [MSG]**

Therefore, if anyone is in Christ, the new creation has come: The old has gone, the new is here! **2 Cor. 5:17 [NIV]**

I f He created me to be in His image, how do I get there? Not that I am there yet, but I am continually changing. Because God loved me and I accepted Him, He took me from nothing but formless clay and is shaping me into a beautiful creation in His hands. He created me into a physical human being and I am being transformed spiritually into His likeness. "And we, ... are being transformed into His image with ever-increasing glory, which comes from the Lord, who is the Spirit" (2 Cor. 3:18NIV). As our transformation and knowledge deepen, the Holy Spirit changes us. My pilgrimage is for my spiritual being to be changed into His Godly image.

We are in God's hands from the beginning of our creation and throughout our whole lives. "fear not, for

I have redeemed you; I have summoned you by name; you are mine" (Isaiah 43:1NIV) Even while He is protecting us, He is allowing irritants, grit, or "circumstances" into our lives to form us into His image. He sees the potential in the sand. Every grain is usable in us. This is the difficult part of being transformed, but sometimes the transformation is more valuable than the outcome here on earth. We do have a refuge in Him while we are being transformed. The sand is easier to accept when we know the beautiful end is more than we can imagine.

Our creation story starts as a thought in God's mind (Jer. 1:5). Before He formed us in the womb, He chose us, He knew us, He consecrated us. Next, He created us. After creation, we have the choice to be "born again." Then the transformation begins. God clings to us, covers us, and leaves His thumbprint on our simple form. We can't stay unchanged; He takes His time changing us and working with us to create a new life in us. "Through Him all things were made; without Him nothing was made that has been made" (John 1:3 NIV). We exist *only* because God made us.

"Being confident of this, that He who began a good work in you will carry it on to completion until the day of Christ Jesus" (Phil. 1:6NIV). The next step allows abrasive grains of sand -bits and pieces of shells and bones, all of which are irritants- into our lives to cause us to change and grow into a gorgeous pearl. He opens the shell just enough to let those pieces into our lives. These grains irritate or hurt us and cause physical and emotional pain. They either strengthen us or we give in to them.

If you give in, you have surrendered to the enemy. Don't give in! In the midst of those grains, if you don't give up, you will gain grit. Eventually, He will be revealed in you and you will become a pearl. The pearl is a created, healed wound that went from nothing, to adversity, to grit, to strength, to a pearl. "For I consider that the sufferings of this present time are not worth comparing with the glory that is to be revealed to us" (Rom. 8:1ESV). God requires grit and adversity to grow us into a marvelous work of completion which will be a prized, cherished pearl.

These grains or pieces are what we define as "suffering." Some of them may be real suffering, but some of them are just enough of an irritant to keep us from getting too comfortable in our shell. Believe it or not, there is a treasure in discomfort and pain. Each grain of sand is created by Him specifically for each one of us, to evoke a specific work in us.

In hindsight, I never really felt like I had a difficult life or suffered. It seems my first real grain was when I was diagnosed with cancer in 2005. Up to that point, I would say my walk as a believer was fairly easy. I had not endured much pain or death in my life or my family's life. I also was not stretched to the point of becoming totally dependent upon Him. I felt extremely blessed even in those times when I thought life was "hard." Blessed, but if I never felt pain or struggled, I would not appreciate those times when life was full of good. My struggles have allowed me to have a new appreciation for life and growing in Him.

I knew immediately this grain of sand from my first bout of cancer would be tough. I had to set my mind on getting well and surviving. As I acknowledged this grain was here for the long haul, I chose to find a plan and get moving toward good health. The doctors gave me a treatment plan. There was to be surgery, chemo-therapy, and radiation. This storm brought many aspects I would need to overcome: physical, mental, emotional, and spiritual for me. I knew it would be hard. I was at peace knowing that I would not die from it, and God had confirmed it to me the night before surgery.

Through my discipline and obedience, God allowed the medical treatments to work to restore me to health. Healthy, with scars, yet healthy nonetheless.

I did not get the "supernatural" miracle I would have wanted, but an abundance of small miracles all worked together to save my life. God gave the doctors knowledge and minds and hands to do what they needed to do. God provided the nurses with knowledge and compassionate hearts to care for me. The cancer grain was not from God, but He allowed it in my life and used that "irritant" to mold me and to use me for His glory. (Isaiah 43:7) He continues to use it every day, and will for the rest of my life, as a reminder to depend on God for every day and every breath. That is what my not getting my supernatural miracle did. It gave me the ability to depend on God every single day.

This storm was mostly a physical battle for me Healthwise. In my heart, I knew I would grow spiritually, as well. The change and growth I see in me is a treasure to me. So, the physical part was won, but it still required me to overcome the spiritual and emotional aspects.

Many of the irritants He allows into our lives that cause us to grow are painful. We may not feel like we are winning the battle. We would rather not have those grains, but there is a positive side to irritants. The grains become grit, and grit is faith, perseverance, strength, and trust-building. My faith grew even in the difficult events I was facing. I never doubted God or questioned Him. I did question why I had to grow. Growing and stretching can sometimes be painful, especially with a grain of sand lodged in you. We must remember our grains of suffering, or burdens, are not worth comparing to the jewel that will be revealed in us someday. (Romans 5:3-5) I also must remind myself, in my weakness, I am made strong and can withstand, because of His covering over me.

God isn't always the one that allows irritants in our lives. Sometimes, by not thinking, we scoop them up ourselves. Regardless of how they get in, He allows us to use them for strengthening us, or for helping us fulfill a purpose. He just repositions us to get us back on track.

Sometimes, grains sneak in on their own, and again, we don't see them coming. He reroutes our path to use them to strengthen us and cause us to grow. God does care about us and doesn't like to see us hurting, but He will use our pain as a great motivator to cause us to look to Him. He will also put challenging consequences in our lives because of our disobedience; even though He forgives our disobedience, there are still consequences. We can still grow. even in our disobedience and consequences. We can still grow if He must reroute us because we took a wrong turn.

Not only must the shell be cracked open, but it must be cracked open *often*. The more grains you overcome, the stronger you become. Just like the paper doll, the more you overcome, the stronger and more beautiful you become. At times, the greater the trial, the greater the impact on those around you. Who you are on the inside begins to change you into a person of greater influence to other people. You have now developed some grit alongside becoming that final pearl. It is, however, a life-long process of changing that makes us the most beautiful pearl. If God doesn't open the shell and permit pieces that allow us to grow to come in, we would effectively be suffocating.

He planned it that the oyster shell will close periodically, and it will open again and again. When the shell does close for periods, it is holding its breath, giving us a rest from sand, a chance to recover before moving on. Press on with your grit! Make it part of who you are, and head for the prized goal of being used by God (Phil. 3:12-14).

Some of my irritants were my father's disease, cancer twice in my body and three surgeries, my mother's mourning and her cancer, homeschooling my daughter -which I don't mean in any negative way-, and other uncomfortable grains of sand. It seemed the grains continued to come at me. Periodically, there was a break to rest, heal, and catch my breath, but not as often as I would have liked.

Everyone has their own sizes and kinds of grains of sand, and different breaks from the sand. Paul's grain was a thorn in his side; Job's grain was immense suffering; David had King Saul as a grain for a while. Some are mental grains, such as jealousy, insecurity, lack of confidence. Some grains of sand also are in our spiritual life, including doubt, discouragement, fear, tiredness, and lack of faith. There also are physical grains, such as illnesses. A grain, no matter what it is, changes us *if* we will allow it to.

"The righteous person faces many troubles, but the Lord comes to the rescue each time" (Psalm 34:19 NLT). When I had to tackle the grain of cancer again this time ovarian-, I felt overwhelmed, to say the least. I thought I had already beaten this "cancer grain" and had learned from it, yet there it was again. At times, it just seemed that either God let in too much sand by opening me just a little too far, or I somehow got a whole mouthful of sand at once.

Did God forget I already used the grain to grow stronger and strengthen my faith? Did He forget other people were equipped better than I was? What was He thinking? Regardless, God is in control, filtering what comes in and out of our lives. He is always in control and right there beside us. "When you pass through the waters, I will be with you; and when you pass through the rivers, they will not sweep over you. When you walk through the fire, you will not be burned; the flames will not set you ablaze" (Isaiah 43:2 NIV). A lot of grains may come into my life. They will never over-flow me or knock me out. He will rescue me every time.

After finishing my chemotherapy from ovarian can-cer, I asked the doctor what my prognosis was. I felt confident because I had managed to do well, all in all. He said, "Let's not talk about that; there's a 95% chance it will come back in the first year." Wow! An-other punch in the gut. And it was not that I had just worked through my thoughts and emotions, but can-cer, surgery, treatment, and the prognosis affect you and your whole family. A year later, I asked him again for a prognosis, because I had made it through a whole year. He said, "Let's wait; there's a 50% chance it will come back in the second year." Statistics can prove whatever you want them to, but only God can prove the truth!

Just because the doctor had his "truth" and stats, didn't mean I had to accept them. I acknowledged them but wouldn't necessarily follow his medical books because God is the one who is always in control. I would follow God. Follow what God says about you. God has the final say and authority over our lives. We must all call on our deepest resource, our God. He's the one who can smash that grain into smaller pieces, so it gets worked into our character. He is the one who has our days numbered and our grains under control. He is the one with the truth and the final say. Listen to the doctor and then cling to what God says.

Mary, who was betrothed to Joseph, had a *big* grain of sand placed into her life. (Luke 1:26-38) The angel announced to Mary she was with a child even before she was married. She was a virgin. For real? What a challenging grain to have to work with. I am convinced she got a rock, not a grain. She accepted that truth at some point and then moved forward doing the best she knew how. She and Joseph did their part in their situation and circumstances. And the most *beautiful* person came from it: Jesus! And He was not just born; he died to save us from our sins. And not only did God use an ordinary, average young girl to give birth to His Son, but her reaction was an example to us. She was wise in choosing so well how to respond to what God had appointed her to do; 2000 years later, she is known for how she moved forward in the birth, life, and death of Jesus. She accepted her grain and moved on. Because she accepted the news doesn't mean it was easy. Today, we are still talking about Mary's amazing testimony. It has rippled down from generation to generation of people, both believers and non-believers. May we manage the grains and tumbling rocks in our own life just as Mary did.

Jonah's grain of sand was the size of a whale! Paul had a grain embedded in his side. Shadrach, Meshach, and Abednego had extremely hot grains of sand! We all have them, some bigger than others.

Our oyster shell never rescues us by spitting out the irritant. It uses the irritant to show His power in our lives. The pearl learns to accept suffering as part of who they are to become. It is just a blip in God's plan for our lives. Eventually, the pearl shows others who God is, because of its luster and physical beauty. The more we endure, the stronger and brighter our core becomes. At times, I had wanted to spit out all my sand and get rid of irritants. In John 16:33, Jesus explains, "In this world, you will have trouble. But take heart! I have overcome the world." I am reminded He is with me and I can overcome.

I have learned to accept my challenges to show others that God is working through me, just as He can work through anybody who is willing. We all must learn to accept the challenges from God that He has allowed into our lives. When life gives you grains of sand, allow Him to use them to make you into a pearl. Make use of the grains bombarding you, and bring glory to God. In time, you will see how grains of sand have changed you for the better. Let Him transform you into your *best* you. The world is watching to see us and how we react to the sand and irritants in our lives. A life that glorifies God with its irritants and sand is a life that reveals God's power and character.

As we begin to take on all the loose sand, we begin to form into a person of strength. "There has never been the slightest doubt in my mind that the God who started this great work in you would keep at it and bring it to a flourishing finish on the very day Christ Jesus appears" (Phil 1:6 MSG). One day, we will reach victory! This work not only impacts our lives so much, but it also reminds us how delicate we are, yet how strong and victorious we are as well.

The pearl is the product of Christ's love for us. The grains have turned our weaknesses into strengths, making our gritty grains of sand into pearls and using our irritants to shape us. Early on, God already imbedded into us some of the grains of sand He is going to allow into our lives to strengthen us. These seasons of adversity (grains) and joys will come into our lives randomly over the years, as we move forward with our daily lives. The grains will become a part of who we are; they become part of our testimony. Being a two-time cancer survivor has become part of my testimony. The focus of our testimonies is not what we have endured, but rather what He has accomplished in us, through our irritants and sand. My focus is not that I had cancer. My focus is what God did in me, what I have learned, and *how* God has used me, despite my grains of sand. Every situation or trial He has and will bring me through equips me for my next grains. The believer will let every grain of sand and every irritant bring honor to God and allow personal growth. It is *all* about Him, *not* about us.

What grains we have in our lives are not the total sum of who we are, either. The way we respond is also part of who we are. We don't get to choose what grains come into our lives. We do get to choose how to re-spond. We do not get to spit them out. I did not ask for the grains of handling dying parents or cancer. They are not who I am, but they are part of my growth pro-cess. I am not defined by my past, my disease, or my flaws. They are an explanation as to why I am where I am, but they *do not* define me. We are defined by Jesus Christ who gave us the power to overcome those hard-ships and help others overcome. They are what molded and shaped me to be able to help others, in whose shoes I have walked. How I responded to them caused me to grow.

Some of the grains are areas in which I feel I am weak, yet because I found strength in God, they reveal God's working in my life. My weak areas cause me to press in closer to Him. When we worship Him, even with the irritants and sand in our lives, our focus be-comes Him, not the sandstorm. Our worship molds the sand into strength and beauty. I will continue to wor-ship Him, despite my sand and irritants. When we en-ter His presence with praise, He enters our circum-stances with power.

Did you ever have one of those days, or even weeks, when you said to yourself, "This is not the life I wanted; I don't like where this is going?" I have, and in those instances, I must say, I didn't always handle the change in my plan well. I didn't want to experience pain and sickness or any trials. Regardless, my experi-ences and grains are still a part of my testimony, whether I wanted them or if I managed them well.

Regardless of the amount of sand or size of my grains, God has and continues to form me. Just because we all have grains in our past doesn't mean we are fin-ished, either. I am sure there are still bits of sand to come. The positive side of irritants is when the love of God flows over us like an ocean wave, not only does it bring grains with it, but it also takes the majority of the sand back with it. The Lord does not leave every difficult irritant in our path to make us work through it. He hears our prayers and takes away a lot of the adversities.

This grain was a life experience of my transformation. Just as they are in you, pearls in me are formed from bits and pieces in to a whole, near-perfect, beautiful gem. He forms us from the inside out. I surrendered my stubbornness to God to transition me from a formless, simple blob to an amazing pearl. Without Him and the process of transformation, I would stay undefined and ineffective. Without God, no amount of determination will transform me into His image. When I was a cluster of cells, He transformed me into a beautiful pearl.

The pearl analogy goes right along with the analogy of the vinedresser, vine and producing fruit in John 15. The vinedresser chooses the seed and the ground. There is a process for that seed to change into a fruit-producing vine. The process is as important as the beginning of being loved and chosen, to the end-product of rich fruit. God can produce fruit in your life, even in your process and tough conditions. God can produce a pearl even in the process and grit of your life.

"United we stand! There is oceanic power in transformation." Ingrid Simmonds

Chapter 4

Formed Through Adversity

Therefore, we do not lose heart.... For our light and momentary troubles are achieving for us an eternal glory that far outweighs them all. **2 Cor. 4:16-17 (NIV)**

I have told you all this so that you may have peace in me. Here on earth, you will have many trials and sorrows. But take heart, because I have overcome the world. **John 16:33 [NLT]**

This grain was about finding joy, contentment, peace, and purpose in my times of adversity. Even believers will have trials here. How could I handle what I was facing and not let it change my beliefs about who God was and is to me? It's easy to wonder about God's faithfulness in difficult times, but our circumstances should never cause our faith to waver. Our faith is in who God is, not in our circumstances. I am only human though, so this grain was a tough one.

Sand is not a curse. It is an opportunity for us to understand more fully who God is and bring us to new levels in our relationship with Him. Sand is formed through adversity. I thought my relationship with God was fine before cancer, but cancer brought a whole new meaning and depth to my walk. I learned lessons I never would have learned, had I not gone through this very difficult struggle. It has helped make me the strong believer I am today.

Our troubles and pain should not diminish our faith. Job went through extreme trials but his faith stood strong. He was extra blessed after he withstood his adversities. There is purpose in trials, pain, and adversity. God tests our faith to reveal how weak or strong we are, and where our heart truly abides. "God withdrew from Hezekiah in order to test him and to see what was really in his heart" (2 Chron. 32:31 NLT).

God knows I worry about health and I don't like pain; both cause me to look to Him and depend on Him every day for the rest of my life. He uses our weak areas to make us depend on Him first, and then to make us strong. Because of how hard my past pains from health issues have been (starting with a tracheotomy at two years old), I tend to be fearful of going to the doctor. I fear they may find cancer again, or some other disease. The thought of it reoccurring would bring me fear. I would lose sleep the night before going to the doctor. Every time some new pain came up, my first thought would go to the worst-case scenario. Satan does a good job messing with our minds. He knows our weaknesses and uses them, especially in our minds. I have to choose to think positively that God is with me and not think negatively that He has deserted me.

I have heard many people say, "God will not give you more than you can handle." I disagree. Yes, He will! If He didn't give us more than we could handle, we would never turn to Him in trust and let Him walk beside us in different seasons. We all face circumstances that are uninvited, unexpected, and jaw-dropping surprises. They cause us to "crash" emotionally and sometimes physically. Even the strongest person will have to face something seemingly impossible. They will face something where the *only* answer is to turn to God. What these difficult circumstances will do to us doesn't stop Him from allowing them. Our faith must be in Him, not in our circumstances. "Those who trust in the Lord are like Mt. Zion, which cannot be shaken but endures forever" (Psalm 125:1 NIV).

These big "crashes" were the trials that caused fear to pop up in my life. What is fear? Fear is a feeling of uneasiness about events going on in our lives. There is a healthy fear that is conditional which protects you. It is a Godly fear. "The fear of the Lord teaches a man wisdom" (Prov. 15:33a NIV). The fear the enemy uses to stop us is an unhealthy fear. The fear that controls your life to some degree (2 Tim. 1:7) is unhealthy. That fear means you have stopped trusting God. My fears were unhealthy. To a certain degree, they were changing the way I lived my life. That kind of fear eventually stops you from the purpose to which God has called you.

We learn to fear those things that have hurt us or scared us in the past. Then, we tend to avoid those kinds of experiences in the future. By avoiding them, we avoid pain and our fear is reduced. The relief I feel by avoiding pain is a strong reward; it reinforces me to avoid certain situations. I am efficient at avoiding doctors. The problem is, avoidance doesn't make the fear or pain go away; I still have to face the issue at some other time. God can be our great pain reliever and fear reducer. We don't have to live with awful, sometimes debilitating fear. David didn't shrink back in fear when faced with battles (I Samuel 17). He asked *first* what to do, then he faced his giants. Jonah was afraid at first, then he ran, and then he was swallowed whole by a whale! He prayed and the whale spat him out (Jonah 1-2). Moses was afraid to confront Egypt's Pharaoh. Prayer and facing their fears were David's, Jonah's, and Moses' greatest weapons.

I have learned and continuing to learn to face my fears and trust God more and more. When we face our pain and fears, we learn to move forward with a different ending next time. "Yet what we suffer now is nothing compared to the glory He will reveal to us later" (Rom. 8:18 NLT). So, the positive side to suffering is nothing compared to what He will show us later.

Suffering, pain, and fear can strengthen our faith and our trust in Him. They equip us to comfort others who are not prepared or have not been schooled to use their pain for good. Pain refines us, produces growth in us, strengthens us, and is nothing compared to our future. Either the enemy uses our pain to silence us, or we allow God to use our pain for the life-changing work which we are capable of. If you've been through it, minister and testify to others in it.

I realize also that not everyone who has pain and suffering gets released from it here on earth. Not all people are healed by God in this life, but His glory will be revealed in them, also. For some, the healing is to go home and live with Him eternally. Some people live with chronic, debilitating pain, sickness, and adversity.

The common question with no answer (at least not yet) is: *Why are some healed but others are not?* Some may ask, "Why isn't God healing me?" The fact that you are not released from pain has nothing to do with your level of faith and spirituality; it has to do with His faithfulness. It means He is faithful to use you as you are.

Your diagnosis and situation may not change. You may not get better, *but* He can still use you. He doesn't need you healed to use you. Those who live with chronic and debilitating pain and still serve the Lord can be used just as mightily as others without those conditions, and have testimonies just as amazing. Look what they do despite their pain. Some day we may have the answer to the questions on healing. In the meantime, He doesn't only use stories and testimonies with happy endings. He uses those difficult, heart-wrenching stories that bring Him glory anyway. He uses those who listen to His voice above other voices.

When I was diagnosed with cancer the first time, I felt such fear, which my family also felt. Along with fear came physical pain through surgery and treatments. Then, in 2013, when I was still cancer-free, I wanted more than anything to avoid cancer in the future so I read up on eating properly, exercising, and whatever else I could find as preventives against cancer. I tried lots of things to avoid re-occurrence. In my mind, I was still facing the mental and emotional fear of cancer. I could not seem to let go of all that "might" happen. I wasn't exactly trusting God but instead trusting the "right things" to keep me healthy.

Real healing begins with trust. I knew that in my heart, but couldn't get my mind to agree. The solution was to have my emotions healed so I could trust God with my future, not to try protecting my future on my own with "worldly" methods. Even amidst all that, I still didn't feel an urgency to ask God, "Why?" It wasn't necessary information I needed to fill my mind or worry about. My thought was, *how are you and I going to handle this God?* My next thought was, *how do people ever do it without Him?* Sometimes, the most painful transformations bring about the greatest healing and the fullest, most beautiful pearl.

At some point, after my first bout with cancer, then my second bout, I became very tired and frustrated with the way stress and fear overwhelmed me. I was studying about healing our hurts and fears. I asked the Lord to show me what from my past was causing this fear. I knew what I was afraid of, but not *why* I was afraid. I wasn't aware of anything in my past that could cause my fear, I was just so tired and ready to be done with my unhealthy fear. I wanted to face my fears like David, Jonah and so many others had done.

One morning, I was doing homework from a study that really spoke to me. I finished my work, then listened to a pastor who gave a sermon about the wounded warrior and the healing of memories. It went along with the study I was doing. He explained how we need to work through pain and fear from our past because it affects our future. Getting past your pain and fear gives you a boost forward to living a better life.

I decided an experience must have occurred in my past that caused me fear and pain from health issues. More importantly, it was affecting my not handling fear of doctors and hospitals now. The Pastor said, "I am going to pray for God to bring to mind memories that require healing," and he began praying. Immediately, a memory came to mind: I was being admitted to the hospital for croup when I was about three or four years old. My father had checked me in and left to go home to the rest of the family assuring me the doctors and nurses would take good care of me. I was choosing the color of hospital gown I wanted when he turned to go home for the night.

Next, my mind jumped immediately to my first day of chemo in January 2006. We had a 40-minute drive to Santa Fe for treatments. I cried all the way there. I was scared but I never understood why I cried so hard and so long. The Lord showed me, through those two visions, that feeling abandoned by my dad was my issue. I wanted my dad there both times to hold my hand and tell me everything would be okay because he was there with me. He left the first time to be with the rest of my family, and when I had cancer, my dad had died only a few days before I was diagnosed. In my mind, he had abandoned me both times when I needed him most.

That "abandonment" hurt me and caused pain I'd been unaware of until those memories hit me. I heard a voice (not audibly) say, "Even though your earthly father unintentionally left you scared and alone, I am here to tell you, you have a heavenly Father. I will never leave you alone or abandoned. I will never leave you or forsake you. I will be with you, no matter what you go through." At that moment, I realized my fear was about being abandoned in my times of great need. I had a fear of being abandoned. I never wanted to be alone in pain.

God's presence gave me peace, just as the voice impressed upon me that I did not need to be fearful anymore. God would be with me in all my pain and adversities. I have been in the hospital many times since and been to countless doctor appointments. I still get nervous about doctors and hospitals, but it is no longer debilitating. No matter what grains come my way, I know He is with me, so outcomes do not matter. He will be there with me.

Now that I knew God would help me overcome, I

could put to rest a lot of my worry and fears about what "might" happen; it no longer mattered. I suspect the vast majority of what we worry about never happens, yet we have wasted time and energy worrying. Healing begins with trust: trust He can heal anything medically, supernaturally or by taking us home. And if He doesn't heal us the way we had planned, do we assume He is not in it or not with us? If we don't believe He can heal, then how will we ever receive healing?

When you are suffering and aware of others who have had a similar experience, there is peace in knowing someone else withstood the storm. They are still standing; they can relate to your storm. This provides you with the courage to move on in your pain and weakness. In 2 Corinthians, Paul talks about being "burdened beyond their strength..." *but* they made it! They withstood the wind and waves. Help others stand through their waves of sand!

It is a great encouragement knowing God's grace is sufficient to see us through. "My grace is sufficient for you, for my power is made perfect in weakness" (2 Cor. 12:9 NIV). If others who are weak endure adversity, we can too! If they move their mountain, I can move mine. His power is within us to march on! He can still bless us at any time, even in our pain.

Ruth's story shows us how to move forward in our pain. Orpah and Ruth were sisters-in-law whose husbands passed away. They were in emotional pain from losing their husbands. Naomi was in pain from losing her husband and two sons. Orpah returned to her family. Ruth stayed and clung to Naomi. They poured themselves into one another's well-being and devoted themselves to helping each other. They moved beyond their brokenness first, and then went forward with their lives. Their past prepared them for their future.

We don't move beyond events in our past, we move forward with them as a challenge we've conquered and can use from this point forward. God fixes our past to fit us into new situations where we make the best use of our gifts and personalities.

If you look around, you will find other people near you who are hurting, fearful, and broken. Some of them believe their lives have been left in defeat or ruins; they believe their lives are over. Discouragement and fear have set in and they can neither see the light at the end of the tunnel nor see a way out. As light, we must show them how many others made their way, endured, and moved on, even in the greatest possible amount of physical or emotional pain.

Sometimes, the enemy tells lies to us in our hurt and pain; he convinces us there is no way through, we are permanently broken, and we are unusable. We give up. We sit in our ruins with our heads hanging down. I believe God showed me He would bring me out of my oppression that had happened during those years. God saw me there and saw how He could pull me up and out, and rebuild or restore me. He didn't see me as I was currently, He saw me as I would be, after being restored. So, brick by brick and one step at a time, God has restored what I believed to be my ruins.

Anybody can be restored. Restoration requires you to work with God. It starts in your mind. Do not believe the enemy's lie that says you are of no use with your pain, fears, scars and ruins or whatever other negative thoughts you are believing. You are still able to be restored and used. God can restore your ruins to a temple. "...you are the temple of God and the Spirit of God lives in you…" (I Cor. 3:16-17) [NLT]

Like humans, the pearl has many enemies in the ocean. Some circumstances cause the pearl to be fearful and stay sheltered in its oyster. The problem is, there would be no growth or change if the oyster stayed clamped shut around the would-be-pearl. So, let Him open up and allow bits and pieces of sand and hardship into your world. He is our shelter, but we also need the wind and rain to make us stronger.

We need to face our enemy. We need the challenge of adversity. Let God be in control of whatever comes in and out of your life. He will protect you and me from our enemies. He will help us work through our fears; He will restore us while strengthening us at the same time.

In hindsight, cancer was totally unexpected and shocking to me. I was pulled from the shelter of God's warmth and comfort and thrown into the cold, harsh ocean of adversity, fear, and gasping for air. I was facing possible death from cancer. I believed it was more than I could handle. I am thrilled to say I grew through adversity and no longer have debilitating fear. Even though I am still not afraid of death, cancer caused me to rethink my life and priorities. Do I live every day as I ought? My days are still numbered. "Teach us to number our days that we may gain a heart of wisdom" (Psalm 90:12 NIV).

My grains of adversity have been part of my testimony. These grains of cancer came fast and hard and I had to deal with them fairly quickly. I was the unadorned, simple form that was flattened by the diagnosis, but I also was willing to be built back up as a testimony of God's power. "But we have this treasure in jars of clay to show this all-surpassing power is from God and not from us. We are hard-pressed on every side, but not crushed, perplexed, but not in despair, persecuted, but not abandoned, struck down but not destroyed" (2 Cor. 4:8-9 NIV). Pain and fear are part of the transformative process. Without Him, there would be no life-giving transformation. Where there is adversity, there is an opportunity for growth. Where there is pain, He is our healer.

> *"God is always there at the shoreline no matter how many times we send Him away."* Ingrid Simmonds

Chapter 5

Worth More Than Rubies

A good woman is worth far more than diamonds.
Prov. 31:10 [MSG]

I have loved you with an everlasting love; I have drawn you with unfailing kindness. **Jer. 31:3 [NIV]**

Facing the hardship of living through cancer caused me to rethink my priorities and who I really am. How much am I worth to Him? Does He really have a plan and purpose for me? Am I still usable? Am I worth saving? These questions caused me to dig within myself and seek Him on a more profound level to find answers. Had I not gone through cancer; would I have learned all those answers? All my (and your) answers are in His Word, but sometimes they are hard to believe. My cancer and struggles didn't change my worth; what mattered was the way I handled them. My answers in His Word changed how I handled the situations centered around my cancer and what I needed to do to survive it. Twice!

Physically, I am here on earth, I know who I am, and above all, I know I belong to Him. I know there is a positive side to all my adversity. Those things I know, but I wish I could grasp the depth of how valuable I am to Him *and* others. I have always struggled to believe I

am precious to God as an individual. I could understand He loved all mankind but not me as an individual.

The enemy had planted lies in my mind that I was
not important; I was not worthy as a person. Those lies
led me to believe I had nothing to share, nothing worth
giving to others. I was plain, boring, average; I was not
someone God would use. It has taken years for me to
work it out in my heart and mind to get to the truth:
He does love me. I am worth more than rubies!

Sometimes our hearts hunger to know we are
loved, valued and important. Sometimes we want
more of Him. Sometimes that hunger is so great, we
accept whatever comes first into our minds. It seems
we've eaten and digested lies from the enemy, or
we've snatched the first answer that comes to mind. In
John 6:48-59, John explains that God is our bread of
life. If anyone eats of that bread, he will live forever.
That is the right food. That is the truth we need to fill
our minds with. Just as you can't shove a meal down
your throat, likewise you can't shove the wrong answer into your mind and heart all at once. Take your
time with God, fully digest all that His Word says to
you, about you.

As the Scripture in Prov. 31:10 says: "Her worth is
far above rubies." I know we are worth even more
than deep blue sapphires, rich green emeralds and,
yes, even sparkling diamonds. We will only become
who He gives us the ability to become in HIS time. If
you go to the pet store and buy a tadpole, you don't go
home and expect it to change into a frog overnight.
God did not give them the ability to change so quickly.

His Holy Spirit does change us if we allow Him to IN

HIS TIME. He will transform our hearts and lives. Although it won't take us millions of years to change, it does take a lifetime to process our changing. The pearl in the oyster shell takes time. Anything of value that is worth having does not appear or occur overnight; it takes its own slow, sweet time. That time is worth spending because our goal is fulfillment in our lives and His fulfillment in ours!

John 3:16-17 declares that God loved us so much that He sent His Son, Jesus, to earth. He lived as a human and walked among us, loved us, ministered to us, served us, and taught us. He experienced whatever we might experience and He experienced it as a human. He loved and served and then His heavenly Father called Him to make the final, excruciating sacrifice for us. God sent Jesus to die for us, to die for our sins. We were worth dying for! What love is more than sending your only son to die for someone else's sins? How awesome is that! We are worth dying for.

And not only did He send His Son, but He sent the Holy Spirit to dwell in us, as well. We must repent, be baptized, and then we will receive the Holy Spirit who will lead us and teach us. "'Repent and be baptized, every one of you, in the name of Jesus Christ for the forgiveness of your sin.' And you will receive the gift of the Holy Spirit" (Acts 2:38 NIV). "But when the Father sends the Advocate as my representative-that is, the Holy Spirit-He will teach you everything and will remind you of everything I have told you" (John 14:26 NIV).

Because of our value to God, He loves us, gives us the Holy Spirit, and brings us from death to new life, from a simple speck of sand to a pearl. Scripture describes how much He loves us, tells us of our worth,

and reminds us how full of His purpose we are. Scripture describes the birds and how significant they are
to Him. They are part of His creation and He takes care
of them. "Look at the birds of the air; they do not sow
or reap or store away in barns, and yet your heavenly
Father feeds them. Are you not much more valuable
than they? Are not two sparrows sold for a penny? Yet
not one of them will fall to the ground outside your Father's care. And even the very hairs of your head are
all numbered so don't be afraid; you are worth more
than many sparrows" (Matt. 10:29-31 NIV).

We are more valuable than birds or all other things
God created, and if He cares for them, how much more
will He not care for us? We are luxurious to God. "For
you are a people holy to the Lord your God. The Lord
your God has chosen you of all the peoples on the face
of the earth to be His people, His treasured possession" (Deut. 7:6 NIV).

Pearls are gemstones exclusively created from another living organism, the oyster shell. The pearl is
created within the oyster. Our God is alive. We are created in His image. "For in Him, we live and move and
have our being" (Acts 17:28 NKJV). Eve was created
from Adam's rib, another living organism. Adam was
alive and both Adam and Eve were created from the
only living God. We are created by the one and only
original, living God.

I have always loved jewelry. I love all gemstones
and to me, the shinier it is, the prettier it is. I could relate to being a pearl when God began showing me how
He was transforming me into one because of my love
of jewels. I usually prefer gemstones, but now I am
seeing pearls from a new perspective. I am also seeing
myself in a new light as an individual full of character,

and a unique pearl. I am beginning to understand and have confidence in my personal value. Notice I said, "beginning to."

Even as I wrote this book, I had put it off and put it off, because there were so many other amazing writers in the world, so many people who had more wisdom than I had. Again and again, though, God kept bringing me back to writing. I was trying to gear up my confidence in God that I did have a story and message to share.

I have Godly confidence, but it's still a struggle. Godly confidence is based on the promises of Christ. "I can do all things through Christ who strengthens me" (Phil. 4:13 NIV). I keep reminding myself of His promises.

I am working to keep up my Godly confidence without giving myself any credit; God deserves all the credit and glory. Nobody, when they have become that pearl is self-sufficient. Nobody became that pearl on their own. Nobody filtered and transformed their grains alone. Everything is first filtered through the hands of God. We are still insufficient people without God (Ephesians 2:8-9). I can do things but I am not self-sufficient. God gives me confidence and He is my source, my confidence and my sustainer.

How does my value compare to the value of a pearl? The value of a pearl is determined a little differently by man's standards. First, we tend to assume incorrectly that sparkling diamonds are the best and most valuable. The beauty of their outside draws us in, but outside beauty isn't the only important characteristic. What is special to God is the heart inside a person after welcoming God's entrance into their life (1 Peter 3:4).

In our world, the value of diamond or any other gem-stone comes from the Four *C's* jewelers use to determine the value of their stones. These Four *C's* are cut, color, clarity, and carat; all of which are physical aspects determining value. God determines our value based on what is everlasting: Our core, our heart, and our relationship with Him.

Cut: The cut of the diamond or gemstone refers to the facet proportions, polish, and the way the gem is cut. In other words, its value is determined from the way man cuts it. Man must intervene to make the gem more valuable than it was when he found it. This means the stone wasn't worth enough when it was found; mankind "improved" upon it to make it more valuable by our standards. We cut and polish it. When we finally place a value and price upon a gem, it is not as it was originally created. Yet, God loves us just as we are and to whom we belong.

Our cut is the "God cut." A pearl is not cut to its round shape. It is formed over years of an irritant (anything that causes a wound) and sand (anything causing discomfort) slowly used in the process to make us a full pearl. In Exodus, God asks that an altar be built with *uncut* stones. Man-made or tool cut stones were unholy to Him. The stones should represent the work of God. To become holy to Him, we are to be "uncut" by man. We are to represent the work of God, not human effort to mold us.

Color: Obviously, our color doesn't matter to God. He loves people of all colors. No single color of a pearl is superior to any other color. It's a matter of taste as to which color appeals to you. Other gemstones are more or less valuable based not only upon their color, but also by their depth of color. Not only that, but a pearl has a whole rainbow of colors in its luster. God loves all colors equally, and I have chosen to see myself as a pure white pearl cleansed by God.

Clarity: This "C" refers to how clear the diamond or gemstone is. If there is no flaw or blemish, it is of greater beauty and value. The higher clarity a diamond has, the higher the magnification required to see its flaws. If that were only true with people! We don't need magnification to find things wrong with ourselves or with other people. Unfortunately, our clarity is not the best anyway. We all have flaws, which others are often quick to see and point out. In God's eyes, we are the clearest of clear. He sees beyond our flaws and sees what we can be. He magnifies our good qualities and uses them. He sees us as flawless and blameless (Eph. 1:4).

A pearl has flaws too, but they are used well to complete the finished pearl, just as God uses our flaws for His purpose in the pearl we become. However, having your flaws pointed out to you is not always bad. You need to know what you need to change. Pointing out the good in you is also beneficial. He has plans for us!

Carat: A carat is the measure of a gem's weight and size. A greater carat amount does not necessarily mean a gem is worth more than one of a smaller carat. In the case of diamonds, quality is worth more than size. The same is true with Christians; more knowledgeable does not mean more worth. A lifetime of accumulating head knowledge doesn't do much for us. We must have a personal relationship with God *first*, then lessons learned will be both head and heart deep.

When I was diagnosed with cancer, the doctors shared their human knowledge and "facts" with me, like where the cancer was in my body, what kind of cancer it was, what stage of cancer I had, stats about it, and the treatment plan. My head was saying, "Here is what I need to do." My heart was saying, "I don't want to hear this or do this." My heart needed to focus on Him, not "be tossed about by the sea's waves." I needed that medical knowledge. I also needed to know in my spirit how I would work through the process. I needed spiritual knowledge. My focus was to bring my thoughts into line with God's Word and grow strong through this trial. That would be a lesson that would last.

So, even though I tried to stay strong spiritually, the head knowledge and facts also played an important role. They must stay in balance. It's our heart quality lining up with our head knowledge and His Word that matters. I was to fight this battle on several levels, physical, mental, emotional, and spiritual. God would transform me through my inner heart as much as through my mind. "But the Lord said to Samuel, 'Do not consider his appearance or his height for I have rejected him.' The Lord does not look at the things people look at. People look at the outward appearance, but the Lord looks at the heart" (1 Samuel 16:7 NIV).

The world's job is not to create, define or place a value upon us; that is God's priority. "Do not conform any longer to the pattern of this world, but be transformed by the renewing of your mind" (Rom 12:2 NIV). The ONLY natural gemstone that has the most value when it is first found, is the pearl. When it is polished and transformed, it is an even more dazzling pearl.

There are also four tests jewelers apply to determine if a pearl is real, and they use more than one test, most of the time. We, too, are given many tests in life to see if we will stand up to those assessments. You cannot fake your way through life as a believer. If you are a believer of the Word, then you will be a doer. "Do not merely listen to the word, and so deceive yourselves. Do what it says" (James 1:22 NIV). If we pass the "tests," we receive a crown, but not just any crown. "Blessed is the one who perseveres under trial because, having stood the test, that person will receive the crown of life that the Lord has promised to those who love Him" (James 1:12 NIV).

Then there's the opposite end of the spectrum from diamonds: fake pearls. Nobody would prefer fake pearls over a genuine set. Being fake or fraudulent is trying to be someone we are not. Imitation pearls are lightweight and have no substance to them; genuine pearls are heavier and have substance (2 Corinthians 11:13-15).

There's no reason for us to put any effort into being someone God didn't create us to be. Be the real you. When we are an imitation, we are worth little and are not created individually. Imitators are made in a plastic "cookie press," and each "cookie" is the same; we would not be made in the image of God, but we would all be mirror images of each other. How boring and unattractive that would be.

We ARE valuable to God. Don't let the world's standards define you and determine whether you are a pearl. Your value does not decrease based on someone else's inability to see your worth. Your worth is based upon what God sees. We are of much importance that God sent His Son to die for us. If we are not being all that God created us to be, then we are not real.

Even before I was a believer, I was worth a lot to Him. I was important to Him but was not able to please Him. "And without faith, it is impossible to please God" (Heb. 11:6 NIV.) Just because I have a different testimony now as a believer, doesn't make me worth more; I have always been valuable to Him. My testimony before was based on external things I did and went through.

Now, it's more about my heart of trust in God and love for Him. I am as valuable as the highest quality pearl to Him. My Artist made me His special masterpiece. When I believed I was worthless, He became my designer and made me of infinite worth to Him! The most important thing is not making me worth it (because I already am); it's about making my life and struggles matter.

"We have His seal of approval." Ingrid Simmonds

Chapter 6

Priceless, Cherished and Irreplaceable

God not only loves you very much but also has put His hand on you for something special. I Thess. 1:4 [MSG]

I'd sell off the whole world to get you back, trade the creation just for you. Isaiah 43:4 [MSG]

Before I had cancer, I had no comprehension of there being no substitute for me. I did not know how unique and individual I was and am. No two people He created are identical. He will protect each one of us because He loves us and because of our uniqueness. God has always had His hand on me, leading me, protecting me, and guiding me. Even though I can't see it, I have felt His hand at times. If I slipped out from under His hand, He would snatch me back.

He would sell off the whole world to get me back and keep me. He doesn't need me, but He chose me and wants me. We are priceless, cherished, and irreplaceable in His eyes. No price is too high for God's people, including me (Isaiah 43:3).

Knowing how valuable I am to Him, the next grain that came my way was learning I was cherished and irreplaceable. There is no substitute for me. In our world today, we have substitutes for many items: foods, art, jewels, stones and pearls, brands of clothing, and even our leaders. There is *no* substitute for Him in our lives. There is also *no* substitute for me as an individual created by Him.

To be irreplaceable means it is impossible to substitute anyone else for you, *even if* you are flawed. Just because you are flawed does not mean you will be tossed aside or someone else will take your place. You are irreplaceable!

A great set of pearls might be replaceable. We certainly are not. Even with your heartbreak and scars, you *are* irreplaceable in God's eyes. If God didn't believe we were irreplaceable, He would not have given up His only Son to save us! Yet He would have died for you or me, even if we were the only ones here.

Matthew 18 tells the story of 99 sheep and the one that was lost. The shepherd searches until he finds that lost lamb. He doesn't say, "Let him go; I will replace him with another sheep." No, that one sheep is very important to the shepherd. You may think it's not critical for Him to go find a particular sheep, but if you're that sheep, it is *very* important to you. There is no substitute for you or me. You are vital as if you were His only sheep gone astray from the ninety-nine.

God doesn't just let us go. He searches until He finds us and continues to care for us. "He is happier about that one sheep than over the ninety-nine that did not wander off" (Matt. 18:13 NIV). Even in our wavering faith and wandering eyes, it does not change who God is or how important we are to Him.

Because we are pre-designed by Him, we have a

purpose for our lives from day one. He has a plan for each of us, and it will be accomplished (Isaiah 46:4). He pre-designed us to be unique in fulfilling His plan. God's desire for us is to stick to His plan. Nobody else has our same combination of creation, gifts, skills, talents, and other attributes.

Only you can be you; only I can be me. We can't be replaced in His plan. He made us each to add to His Kingdom as only each of us can. "For we are God's handiwork, created in Christ Jesus to do good works, which God prepared in advance for us to do" (Eph. 2:10 NIV).

Jesus handpicked 12 unique disciples. He didn't need disciples. He wanted disciples. Having disciples gave Him people with whom He would have close relationships. Each of them was very different with different personalities, strengths, talents and yes, even flaws. They were His followers who were to do His work with Him on earth and after He had ascended. Together, they worked to serve God's purpose here on earth (Co. 3:23-24). There was no substitute for any disciple who wasn't going to follow Jesus that day. He needs each of us. For all eternity, across the earth, there is not another one as unique as each of us.

Psalm 139 says we are fearfully and wonderfully made. When we entered the world at birth, we changed it because we are uniquely who we are and we arrived here at a specific time and place. We each bring a unique personality, skills, and presence that no other person brings. We bring our own conglomeration of characteristics. We bring unique relationships that bless us and others.

At the same time, each of us is like a puzzle piece,

unique and pre-designed to connect in the big picture. We are all part of a bigger picture. Somebody else could fit in my spot, but it might not prove to be the best fit. You fit like that unique puzzle piece. The bigger picture is, piece by piece, how we show the world God is alive and loves us all because of our differences.

In Exodus 4, God asks Moses to be Israel's deliverer and to speak to the people. God planned to use Moses specifically and didn't want to use somebody else. He didn't want to find a replacement. Moses tries to convince God he is *not* the one God should be using. He doesn't believe the people will listen to him. "They won't trust me. They won't listen to a word I say" (Ex. 4:1 MSG). And even after God shows Moses why they will listen, Moses argues he isn't a talented talker. There were others who would work better. God gets angry with Moses for not being obedient. "I'll be right there with you-with your mouth! I'll be right there to teach you what to say" (Ex. 4:12 MSG). Moses further argues with God but God was patient with him. Eventually, Moses comes around to being obedient to Him and God assigns Aaron to Moses as a helper.

How could we even think to argue with God? Did Moses trust God, or were his questioning and arguing masking Moses' lack of trusting what God asked him to do? What pride causes us to think we know better than God? What pride causes us to even question God? If we question God, then we do not totally trust Him. Our calling can't be fulfilled that easily if we continually question God. Our ministry or calling also cannot best be filled by somebody else. A substitute wouldn't do the job as well as who God called for that task.

God needs us to do what He has called us to do, not to question Him. He never asks us to do what He doesn't supply us with the ability to do. "And God is able to make all grace abound to you, so in all things at all times, having all you need, you will abound in every good work" (2 Cor. 9:8 NIV). Moses was the one God handpicked to speak to the people. Don't hide behind your insecurities and lack of confidence; look to God who gives you the ability, without question.

As part of the Scripture in Isaiah God showed me, verse 4 also says He chose me. He impressed upon me that <u>nobody</u> could be a substitute for me. I learned if I loved Him, continued to serve Him, and did what He asked of me, I would survive cancer to have an impact on the lives of my children and grandchildren. My motivation to get well then became one of living long enough to meet and know all my grandchildren and being a Godly legacy for them. God is priceless to me; I can teach that to my grandchildren. Daily, I am also choosing to be obedient. I am doing one thing at a time as He asks me. Ability because of obedience is a legacy I choose to share with future generations and He will honor that.

I always thought God could easily find a substitute for me. I think there are others around who are better suited to do His work than I am. What *I* think doesn't matter. What matters is that God knows what I am best suited to do. The lie the enemy always planted in my mind was that others are more usable by God.

The more I know God, the more I see my uniqueness, and the more I understand that nobody else is like me. No set of "fake" pearls will replace a genuine, complete set. I am one-of-a-kind and He will never replace me with another. We must learn to embrace our uniqueness and value and follow through with obedience to Him.

Pearls are priceless, unique, and cherished; they cannot be replaced with imitation copies. Without Him, I am ordinary and replaceable, but with Him, I am extraordinarily and uniquely usable. When I was unworthy, He made me worthy.

"Sea your beauty and worth in Christ." Ingrid Simmonds

Chapter 7

Comparing Gemstones and Diamonds to Pearls

For we are not bold to class or compare ourselves with some of those who commend themselves; but when they measure themselves by themselves and compare themselves with themselves, they are without understanding. 2 Cor. 10:12 [NIV]

Make a careful exploration of who you are and the work you have been given, and then sink yourself into that. Don't be impressed with yourself. Don't compare yourself with others... Gal. 6:4 [MSG]

The next grain in my life was not a new grain, it was the comparison grain. I have always compared myself to others but never managed to find myself as "worthy" as others. Comparison for the wrong reasons is harmful. It could be a comparison of looks, possessions, spiritual gifts ... whatever you are looking at that is someone else's, that you wish you had for yourself. Upon learning of *my* value and importance to God, and seeing how He could use me, I was led me to see there was no reason to compare myself to others.

Who I am to others is not important, who I am to

Him is all that is important, along with who He is and how my uniqueness can bring glory to Him. It's not even about who I am at this point, it's about who I will be at the finish line. We will all stand on the same, level ground on judgement day.

Diamond is considered the strongest, hardest, natural material on earth. Man must chisel down to find a diamond. On the other hand, pearls are soft and every layer builds up to make pearls stronger. People chisel down, but God builds up. I wouldn't want to be strong on my own. If I were strong on my own, I would never learn to rely on God. There is no point in comparing diamonds to pearls. They are not created the same, nor made of the same material. One wears down, another builds up. God has made many diamonds but I am one, unique pearl.

Pearls cannot be compared; they are in a class by themselves. One of the biggest problems I see among women is that they tend to compare themselves to other women, and always seem to come up short in some areas; as a result, they don't pursue relationships or participate in the Body. They stick to themselves in their belief that they are nothing compared to others and have nothing to offer.

We cannot compare ourselves to others. There is no reason to compare because each person is in a class of their own to God. People are unique from other creatures and each person is unique from every other person.

"We're not putting ourselves in a league with those who boast that they're our superiors. We wouldn't dare do that. But in all this comparing and grading and competing, they quite miss the point." (2 Cor. 10:12

MSG). We must compare ourselves only according to God's standards. Measuring ourselves by one another instead of by God's standards is a sin. When we continually try to measure ourselves with others and are compared by others, we aren't accepting who God made us to be. Such comparisons produce all kinds of characteristics that *are not* from God and can produce inferiority, insecurity, or feelings of rejection, pride, anger, greed, and/or selfishness in us.

If you compared yourself to God, which seems silly, hopefully, you would be discontented with who you are and find the desire to allow the Holy Spirit to change you and make you more like Him. "To whom will you compare me? Or who is my equal? Says the Holy one" (Isaiah 40:25 NIV).

Don't measure yourself by looking at someone else's life. Usually, when we look at someone else, chances are, what we're seeing on the outside is not necessarily representative of what's on the inside. In that sense, we're comparing ourselves to who we *think* they are. Don't set limits on what God will do in your life based on what *you think* He did and continues to do in other people's lives. I don't compare myself to anyone now, because I am not them, I am not who and what I was, and I'm not yet all I will be.

One day, I was at the bank to pay off the used Porsche I had just bought. It was my splurge with some of my inheritance from my mother's estate. After briefly chatting with the teller, she excitedly said, "How nice to be able to pay off a Porsche!" I'll admit it felt good to buy a dream car and be able to pay it off right away. "I wish I was you and had your life," the teller said. *No, Miss, you really wouldn't wish you were me. If you only knew* .... was my thought. What she didn't know was that my mother had passed away. She didn't know I was dealing with cancer daily, paying for two children in college, and so on. She had no idea of the stress and anxiety in my life. She had "known" me for only five minutes, and her comparison of my life to hers was based only upon what she knew about me in that instant. Five minutes of my life was all she knew and she was envious.

Often, we see the five minutes in people's lives. Our world of Facebook and hashtags looks perfect in the one fingerposts of our lives, summed up in what we want the world to see and know. Most of the time, people show the world their best sides and the times that make them look like they have a great life. They don't show you who they really are, or what mountains stand in their way. I could have told the teller my "real" story. I could have told her about my parents having cancer, the financial struggles of putting children through college, worrying about cancer returning, my fear that people didn't accept me, and I could have gone on and on. I'm sure she had struggles of her own which she could have shared with me.

We never know what valleys or hilltops or oases other people are in, but if we really knew who they are inside, or what mountains they are trying to move, chances are, we wouldn't find any reason to be jealous. When we are really close to someone, chances are we aren't jealous of them because we do know their whole story. We don't wish we could experience what they've experienced. We would not wish our problems upon them either.

The enemy's target is our mind through the ways he leads us to compare ourselves, and the insecurity that follows. His weapon is those lies that creep in, filling our minds with dirty lies that downplay ourselves. Paul says in Romans 2:11 that, our greater weapon is the truth and His truth will set us free. Insecurity is the fear of not being accepted the way we are by others.

The world pushes us to believe we are inferior if we don't acquire "status" or riches. We are pushed to be "Number 1." Don't conform to the world's standards. Don't make lower your worth. Know you are safe in God's eyes. You are of the highest worth and important to Him where you were, where you are, and where you will be.

Comparison sometimes produces the opposite of inferiority; that is superiority or pride. We look at our wonderful selves, we puff ourselves up with pride, and then believe we have reached a higher status. If we compared ourselves according to God's standards all the time, we would see there is not much to be proud of. There is no basis for our pride. All we own, all that we are, and all that we will ever be is because of Him. No one person is better than another in God's eyes. (ROM. 2:11) Nothing we carry has been completed through our own power and ability. If you must give credit to someone for your success and "stuff," give the credit and the glory to God!

"Get rid of all bitterness, rage and anger, brawling and slander, along with every form of malice" (Eph. 4:31 NIV). Comparison produces bitterness, anger, or resentment towards others and God, as well. The more "why don't I have this or that" you voice out and believe about yourself, the more your anger and frustration build. There is anger for what you wish you were and frustration for what you don't have. Nobody is perfect or complete. We all fall short in some area. God doesn't give you what you think you want; He has a better idea and has a better way to fill your desires.

Comparison causes greed and selfishness as you begin to falsely believe what you already possess and your abilities are not enough. You are not content; you want more, more, more. This breeds ingratitude; it is saying, "I don't like what God gave me or how He made me." When we label ourselves as "poor," "unlikeable," "unusable," or just "not enough", we are making an unfair judgment about what God has planned for us before He is finished with His work in us. It causes us to be greedy and want more.

Don't become discontented with who you are, your life position and your possessions. That greed and selfishness will lead to destruction. "People who want to get rich fall into temptation and a trap and into many foolish and harmful desires that plunge men into ruin and destruction" (1Tim. 6:9 NIV). Learn to distinguish wants from needs. Be content without having all you want. Choose to be content with who God made you, in what He has given you, and in how He is changing you.

Comparison takes your focus off God and puts it on you. Have you ever sat in a room, looked at the ceiling and noticed one ceiling tile is missing? Your gaze tends to focus on the hole where the tile is missing, as opposed to all the other tiles hanging up there perfectly straight. The more you focus on the one that is missing, the more it is magnified in your mind.

To avoid comparing yourself with others (the missing tile), try keeping your focus on God and the bigger picture of who He made you be and all the ways He has blessed you. If our focal point is our problems, we will be overwhelmed or overcome with discouragement. If we see the whole picture from God's perspective, we will know we can have victory.

Comparison causes jealousy. "For where you have envy and selfish ambition there you find disorder and every evil practice" (James 3:16 NIV). Comparison is a situation with no winner. In the world's eyes, you are insufficient, a loser, not a winner. Don't let the world pressure you and tell you that you are insufficient. In Christ, we are sufficient! May your faith not rest in the thoughts and words of men but the power of our God. "He said to me, 'My grace is sufficient for you, for my power is made perfect in weakness'" (2 Cor. 12:9 NIV).

He made us who we are and designed us exactly as He planned. He sees tremendous potential in each of us. If we are obedient to Him and allow Him to have authority over our lives, we have placed ourselves in His hands. Don't give in to the temptations of jealousy and comparison.

Comparison is not just comparing physical looks; it also is spiritual. Each pearl is unique in characteristics and each pearl fits side by side and enhances each other. Each of us is characteristically unique, but side by side we fit to help enhance one another and help fulfill God's plan. Your characteristics are just as relevant as that of another person. No one person's characteristics, personality, abilities, gifts are greater than any other's.

It is not your ability that matters, but your "availability". Many people in the Bible were mightily used by God and were not greater than anybody else. They were just obedient and did what God asked of them.

If you look closely enough at a pearl, you will always find some sort of imperfection. They each possess their own flaws, but flaws don't stop a jeweler from using them. He works with them until they look their best. There will always be some imperfections in us, yet there is also good in all of us. We all have our flaws, and yet, we are still usable by God *if* we are willing to be changed.

A flaw is a gift from God reminding us He can still use us, no matter what. God works with us until we become more like Him. "Be perfect, therefore as your heavenly Father is perfect" (Matt. 5:48 NIV). Someday we will all be perfect, even as Christ is perfect.

On a deeper level, my hardest battle with comparison concerned a different kind of comparison; I was not comparing myself physically to others but comparing my cancer to the cancer journeys of others. I was listening to statistics on cancer survivors and how long they lived with it, lived in remission, how much time they had before it returned, or how long before it claimed their lives. I was trying to comprehend where I fit on their projections and charts. Doctors hypothesize with lots of statistics and probabilities to tell you what they think you should hear. I realized none of that mattered.

God's timetable is not theirs. He is the final decision maker in all of that. Ultimately, I didn't fit into their statistics. After the first year, they told me I was a "super responder." That wasn't what they expected. I hadn't fit into the medical statistics and formulae. God doesn't fit into our statistics either. He is all-powerful and the designer of His own charts and formulae.

Comparison is a hard layer for me. I have to remind

myself daily that we all have different strengths and weaknesses, so there is nothing that says I should compare myself to others. The layers that complete me as a person are unique to me. Your layers are different from mine. I must focus on the Creator, not the other creations.

Just as no two pearls are alike, no two people are alike; yet we try to come up with a list of characteristics and abilities trying to feel like we are equal to someone else. Even worse, we want to feel like another person and be superior to someone else. We assume others are more knowledgeable or powerful, and we want that. The best way to feel good about yourself is to serve one another. The rewards of serving are so much greater than a feeling of superiority because that feeling has no basis except selfishness. Each one of us is significantly different in looks and characteristics. We all have different genes that God chose specifically for us.

You cannot compare to yourself anything that seems better in someone else. Our decisions in comparing each other are subjective. God's objective for each of us is to be unique and complete persons found whole in body, mind, soul and spirit. It's not what you achieve or who you look like that brings Him joy, but rather who you are, uniquely to Him. When my focus was on others, God helped refocus my eyes fully on Him.

"Avoid comparison and peer pressure." Ingrid Simmonds

Chapter 8

Breakable but Valuable

He heals the broken hearted and binds up their wounds. **Psalm 147:3 [NIV]**

Heart-shattered lives ready for love don't for a moment escape God's notice. **Psalm 51:17 [MSG]**

Even before cancer (in my 40's), the lie that my mind would believe was that I was too old to be used. God needed to use newer, fresher Christians who had withstood tough times. I also believed that I was not a person with much life experiences and challenges to justify my being able to share with others how to handle life's struggles. I have to daily remind myself that God will use ANYBODY willing at any age and/or stage of life. Many of the people used mightily by God in the Bible were older.

Cancer did cause me to become more aware of my mortality, but it also gave me a fresh perspective on priorities, what is truly a priority and what is not. Being used by God is a priority. I am valuable and do have something to share. He has shown me through others that I am still usable and have something important to share.

After coming through cancer, I was spending too much time worrying about whether it would return. I know He had spoken to my heart with a word that I would be fine, but I would forget that. Sometimes, we tend to believe the doctor's report instead of God's report. We lose our focus and forget what God told us. I was thinking, *There is not much for me to do here except work to keep the cancer from returning.* I totally left God out of "my plan." Because my focus was so blurry then, I was *not* usable. My grain was to change my focus from broken and unqualified to restored, chosen, and qualified.

We're kind of like a watermelon, hard on the outside but looks pleasing to the eye. If you were to break open the watermelon, it would no longer be whole. But in its brokenness, the inside is sweet, juicy, and filling. It's refreshing in a way. The watermelon is more usable broken than whole. So, sometimes, God can use us in our broken state as opposed to being whole.

People and watermelons are still usable in their brokenness. God doesn't wish to replace us with someone else and He doesn't want us to be fragmented and broken from life's pain, but He can use us either way. Watermelons are mostly water and water gives us life, so if you are broken, you are still full of water and life. And, after you've been broken and used, you are left with a seed and story to share with others. You can choose to let God use your brokenness.

A definition of broken is to be divided by force. Sometimes life circumstances break us by the sheer weight and force of them. Those times will most likely leave scars but God uses those scars too. Scars don't ever go away but they get easier to look at and become accepted as part of our testimony. They have an important story to tell.

God uses whole individuals but will take people with hearts broken for Him. He will use anyone willing to be used, regardless of their condition. People regardless of their scars can be used. If you break a pitcher and you never fix it, it is permanently broken. You could just replace it. If you glue it together, it is still usable, even with its scar. It takes more work to be restored than just replaced. God is the great restorer. He will make us beautiful again, use our history for a testimony, and also create a new story in us. God will lead you out of your brokenness *if* you will only let Him. "He heals the brokenhearted and binds up their wounds" (Psalm 147:3 NIV). God is the God of healing and restoration! He makes all things new and beautiful.

Usually, more than one situation or circumstance bring about our brokenness. For me, cancer and my father's death were pulling me in two directions. Circumstances can pull us away in more than one direction. Sometimes we are only broken just a bit; other times, the weight crushes us into a heap of powder. Regardless of how broken you feel, He desires to still use you.

Satan loves for us to believe we are broken to the point of being unable to be used or restored. He strives to break us one way or another, but God loves to restore us to wholeness. 1 Peter 5:10 says, "After you have suffered a little while, the God of all grace, who has called you to His eternal glory in Christ, will himself restore..." (NIV).

When you see or feel like a pile of broken pieces, remember that He takes broken pieces and restores them. Crushed pearls are much harder to piece back together but they are still usable. God can restore anything! "Therefore, if anyone is in Christ, the new creation has come: The old has gone, the new is here" (2 Cor. 5:17 NIV). Even if He doesn't restore you physically, He can restore you spiritually. He can use you regardless of what your physical state is. Your spiritual restoration, though, is of utmost importance.

So how does God use a crushed pearl? The Chinese have been crushing pearls for centuries. They crush them to use in cosmetology products. Whole pearls are silky, smooth, and radiant. They reflect light. So, the Chinese reasoned, if you crush pearls and put them in facial and skin products, they will create a face that will glow and look "exquisite and opulent". Crushed pearl-powder applied to the face became a symbol of opulent wealth in China. Such a face would reveal beauty by reflecting the light in a soft, peaceful glow. If the wealthy invested in crushed pearls, then our rich, heavenly Father would certainly invest in us, knowing we would reveal His beauty, light, and peace exquisitely, *even* in our crushed state!

For those days when you can't see past your heap, God takes your hand and gently brushes aside the heap to make room for what else He can do. God doesn't see us how we are right now; He sees how He can restore us or how we are to be used. Slowly, He works with us, restoring us to wholeness. When something is restored to wholeness, it does not mean that object or person is perfect; it just means the object or person is still usable in its entirety.

If we are in Him, we qualify as usable. God is the powerful substance in our crushable, fragile lives. He supplies the power and the strength to endure. Because He chose us, and we are in Him, we are qualified.

How do we help someone else seemingly suffocating beneath their heap? Get down there with them and let them see your scars. Our scars can be the glue to help piece others back together. Share with them about the time when you had to reach up to touch bottom. Pray with them. Read the Word with them. God will work through the Holy Spirit, your prayers, your actions, and your testimony. "The Spirit of the Sovereign Lord is on me, because the Lord has anointed me to proclaim good news to the poor; He has sent me to bind up the brokenhearted..." (Isaiah 61:1 NIV).

God calls us to help one another and lift these burdens. God loves them and will still use them. Show one another how to mend your pieces back together again. "Carry each other's burdens, and in this way, you will fulfill the law of Christ" (Gal. 6:2 NIV) God never intended for us to be crushed to the point of death, and He uses relationships with Him and others to restore us.

After going the distance with cancer twice, and working on accepting the changes in my body and all the many scars, I had to adjust my thinking. I was thinking I looked like a quilt full of scars. Who would want this body? Who wants to look like that? Who can be used like that either? Even the most tattered quilt will provide some warmth and meet a need.

So, yes, I am covered with scars and still have wounds from working my way through the mountain of grains put in front of me, but I will still fulfill what God has assigned my heart to do. With all my scars, I will be a comforter to help someone else on the same path. I am still usable. All of us have scars, some are just bigger or more evident than others. Pearls have scars of sorts, or flaws, as we sometimes call them.

Some you see and others are hidden, but they are all usable and are a symbol of your strength. "Don't let the enemy define you by your scars. Jesus wants to define you by His."[2] Jesus' scars preached a very powerful story that nobody could deny. My scars also tell a powerful story.

When I speak of being restored and whole, I am not necessarily referring to physical wholeness, but also spiritual wholeness. You might be physically whole and crushed spiritually. In that condition, you are extremely difficult to use, but there is still hope for you. Your spiritual condition must begin the healing process first, yet, you can even be used at the same time you are healing. Spiritual healing is cleansed by the blood of Jesus. Next, protect that wound by renewing your mind, and remember, after being healed, scars are not there to remind us of the pain, but to remind us of where we have come from and that we have been healed.

Did you know the pearl is the only gem that cannot easily be cut and still maintain its purpose? Its purpose was to be whole and used. If it is cut, it crumbles. Is it still usable? Yes, it just has a new purpose. Has the enemy cut you to your core? If you are not restored to wholeness, you are still usable. As powder, a pearl can

---

[2] Giglio, Louie. https://www.sermonquotes.com; retrieved July 25, 2017; https://sermonquotes.com/louie-giglio-2/12316-dont-let-the-enemy-define-you-by-your-scars-when-jesus-wants-to-define-you-by-his-louie-giglio.html?fbclid=IwAR2Bt--cJW1EwxeEfggeYb7DVFhDzFm08sYXdvmclB9yVhgnvmfFeWNHN64

still be used to reveal the light of Christ. If you cut any other gemstone, you just make it a smaller piece. Remember your healing and not your pain.

Christ is stronger than anything that could break or crush us. Pearls are beautiful whole and alone, but a set connected in harmony is even more beautiful. A pearl that reveals the light of Christ also is an exquisite beauty. Let Him make you whole.

"Waves may break on the shore but you will be sea-habilitated." Ingrid Simmonds

Chapter 9

Compassion and Care for His Pearls

Be shepherds of God's flock that is under your care, watching over them-not because you must, but because you are willing, as God created you to be; not pursuing dishonest gain, but eager to serve; not lording it over those entrusted to you, but being examples to the flock. I Peter 5:2 [NIV]

When working as a caregiver, wife, and mother, I wanted others to take care of me, have compassion on me, and give me a break. Some people helped, but not as much as I felt I needed. This grain helped me to realize in order to receive care and compassion, I needed to learn to ask for it and accept it. Then, because I knew what it felt like, I would remember to help in the future. After I recovered, I looked to find others lacking the compassion and care they needed and meet that need for them. It was more about doing what God asked of me than anything. Don't let your focus be on meeting a need, let your focus be "what would Jesus do?" Jesus is our greatest example of compassion and care. I now realize I must always be on the lookout for others in need of compassion.

"Be kind and compassionate to one another." (Eph. 4:32a NIV). When we have compassion, we have sympathy and feel for someone else's troubles, thereby wanting to release them from their trials. The Bible instructs us to have that kind of compassion and to take care of one another.

A friend called me one day and told me she worked with a young lady in her 20's who had been diagnosed with Stage 4 cancer similar to mine and didn't have much time. Her mother had passed away fairly recently from cancer and her father was in poor health. She didn't know if the young lady was a believer or not, but she knew I could relate to her situation. I could be *used*! She asked if I would email the young lady. I began to email her and write her letters. I encouraged her, gave her Scriptures and prayed for her. I told her God's plan for salvation. Through the months, I never had a response and I never met her. She passed away and still no word from her. It didn't matter to me. She needed emotional care and someone who could relate to her emotional needs.

I won't know in this lifetime, if the young lady accepted Him. I rest secure in the fact that I did what Jesus called us to do. I did my best to show her the way. We need only do what He asks and ask Him to bless the rest. I had compassion for her in her hopelessness. "When He saw the crowds, He had compassion on them, because they were harassed and helpless, like sheep without a shepherd" (Matt. 9:36 NIV). Jesus was the ultimate example of compassion and He takes care of us.

Awareness that an object or a person needs care and compassion requires us to open our eyes. Some can't or won't ask for help, so we must keep our eyes open. When we do see someone who requires attention, our compassion should move us to action to care for them. Caring is essential in making pearls last a lifetime. Just like pearls, to endure, it is essential to care for one another.

"In the same way, faith by itself, if it is not accompanied by action is dead" (James 2:17 NIV). When people are hurting, our actions may speak louder than our words. The faith of people who are hurting may not be strengthened by what we say, but it will be strengthened because we acted. Actions do speak louder than words. Our actions are not a substitute for our faith in Christ, they are a confirmation of our faith. Our actions should not be performance-driven but passion-driven. Show love and put action with it.

"If anyone has material possession and sees his brother or sister in need but has no pity on them, how can the love of God be in that person?" (1 John 3:17 NIV). I am sure there are many other believers in our churches and our circles near us who are hurting. Their grains are causing pain in their lives. They are lonely, fearful, and hurting, just as I was. For some reason, we seem to always assume we're the only ones trudging on a treacherous path full of rocks and thorns. We're the only ones being bombarded with sand. Yet, there is always someone trying hard to tackle an issue or challenge, whether it is physical, spiritual or emotional. As a friend, I can reach out to them, lift them and walk beside them as they struggle with their sand.

Maybe the hurting person is in your neighborhood or at work. Maybe one of us in our circle of believers is the hurting or broken one. Learn to reach out to help when you see the need. Learn to receive help if you are the one who is hurting. Strive to accomplish God's desire to take care of ourselves and others. Care for others with joy and eagerness, not out of obligation.

You must take care of yourself first because you never know when someone will need you. If you are already taken care of, then you are well-placed in a position to care for others. When you have overcome your "mess," you will have a message to share with someone else whose path you have walked on. However, even a person in the center of their mess still can be used just as you can be used in your troubles.

How do we know if someone needs our care, compassion, and attention? Everyone requires compassion to one degree or another. Everyone has a need. Some may be small and not require much attention. You may already have a suspicion that someone has needs. Sometimes you just have to open your eyes, your spiritual eyes, too. "Is anyone among you sick? Let him call for the elders of the church, and let them pray over him, anointing him with oil in the name of the Lord" (James 5:14 NIV). Don't assume the sick are healing. Don't assume they are enduring their grains just fine. Pray for them anyway and question how they are doing.

I found out also, that those who appear to be the strongest often require the most attention at times. So many people have said to me, "You're so strong, you'll get through." Those words of encouragement are great and I appreciate them, but just because I am strong doesn't mean I don't have weak moments. I still desire a friend at times. Sometimes I don't want someone to do anything but be there to rejoice with me when I rejoice and weep with me when I weep. We all have our weak moments or bad days. Make it a point to ask even the strong people if they are doing well. Don't just take care of the people who are in obvious need.

How many people missed the encouragement they were longing for today because one of us didn't do what He asked of us? We have a monthly ladies fellowship at our church. There are a few ladies who don't come at all. I asked a particular lady why she didn't ever come, and to my surprise, she replied, "I don't get anything out of it and it doesn't meet my needs." Why does it always have to be about us? The woman may not have been fed by our fellowship, but maybe she had insight she needed to share with someone else. Her message or testimony might have been exactly what someone needed to hear. Maybe she *was* the answer to someone else's prayer.

It isn't always about what we think we need or want, but about helping and feeding others. We must open up and let the Holy Spirit use us. A lot of times when we are sharing and helping someone else, the Holy Spirit automatically meets a need without our realization of it. Don't waste your life experiences and testimony by keeping them to yourself. Learn from your storm and how to be ready for the next storm and share your storm. Put your umbrella up over others. Don't keep your mouth shut when you should open up and share and encourage them. Let your words become the hope to encourage the wounded on life's pilgrimage. Be prepared to share that living hope that lies within you!

We also cannot assume those in the church, even in our close circle, will be able to read our minds. We can't always know what is going on in somebody's life. If we sit quietly, our needs won't be met. You must open up to communicate your needs to at least one person. We must overcome our fears that others will label us as weak or that we're a burden because we need help or encouragement. Maybe it's a control issue. God is the only one who should be in control of us. You might fail to ask for help when you need it because you are embarrassed or afraid you will be told nobody can help you. Sometimes, though, you are being prideful and pride is a sin. In Exodus chapter 18, Moses was trying to do too much on his own. He assumed he could do everything on his own. With the advice from his father-in-law, he learned he could delegate others to help him. With help, he succeeded. We must learn to trust the body, ask for help and be aware others are available to minister. All we need to do is ask for help.

In John 4, Jesus told the Samaritan woman He had water that whosoever drank of it would never thirst again. He was referring to a spiritual drink so she would never thirst again. He met both of her needs. There are spiritual hunger and thirst in our world today. Hunger and thirst are needs that require care. We have the spring of water to share with those who are spiritually hungry and thirsty. We have the opportunity to share a sip of one-time encouragement or by being a mentor who continuously and regularly fills others. Our care and compassion meet that need for others.

Ecclesiastes 4:9-10 [NIV] says, "Two are better than one because they have a good return for their labor: If either of them falls, one can help the other up. But pity anyone who falls and has no one to help them up." Help one another get up and move on in the hard times.

In caring for my parents, myself, and my daughter, I was the physical, emotional, and spiritual caretaker.

I didn't feel like I had anyone who was helping care for me and my physical, emotional or spiritual needs. Every day was a struggle. I wanted care in every area of my being. Who else needs that now? How many other people are there who need to be encouraged?

Just as we pay special attention to pearls, some people require more attention than others, especially those who are easily crushed, defeated, or already broken. "Not looking to your own interests but each of you to the interest of others" (Phil. 2:4 NIV). Again, your testimony comes into play here. What better time to share how you withstood a difficult season in your life. Let them know you experienced what they are trying to overcome. The goal is not only to show them how to walk those challenging paths, but also to remind them of what God is doing in them, through them, and will do in their future. Your story meets a need.

Healthy pearls must be worn periodically to keep their luster and to keep them vibrant. When believers become dormant and unused, they too die a spiritual death. We must strive to take care of our gifts by using them regularly. When God calls you to accomplish a task, chances are it will be by using your gifts. If you are called by Him, respond with obedience because you are chosen. "For many are invited, but few are chosen." (Matt. 22:14) [NIV] If we don't respond to our calling as part of a body or relationships, chances are somebody else will step up and do it. We will be replaced and miss a blessing.

We must accept compassion and care, as well as be compassionate in our care of others. Compassion is an example to the world of Christ's love and how He cares for us. If you have experienced the blessing of God's compassion and care for you, show someone else the same attention and bless them. Learn also to accept it in your own life.

"Do nothing out of selfish ambition or vain conceit. Rather, in humility place the importance of others above yourselves, not looking to your own interests but each of you to the interests of the others." (Phil 2:3-4) [NIV]

This grain is learning not only how to accept compassion from others, but also how to extend Christ's compassion. I learned how I could be compassionate toward others who were in the same boat I had been in. Whatever others said or did for me that made me feel cared for, I can do for others. Those 10 years were not easy for me. There was a lot of physical pain, as well as emotional pain. I hope I always have just enough of a twinge of pain to remember what it was like, so it causes me to stay compassionate toward others who are hurting in our world.

It is very important to take care of precious pearls. In fact, pearls thrive when they are cared for. We too, must be taken care of and take care of others as He takes cares of us. Without Him, we fall apart. When I needed care, He was watching over me.

"Let your worries drift away, God will take care of you and keep you in ship-shape." Ingrid Simmonds

Chapter 10

Shining Light to the World

Do all things without grumbling or arguing, so that you may become blameless and pure, "children of God without fault in a warped and crooked generation. **Phil 2:14-15 [NIV]**

In the same way, let your light shine before others, that they may see your good deeds and glorify your Father in heaven. **Matt. 5:16 [NIV]**

At the beginning of my treatments, I was seeing myself as unloved, unusable and of no value. But now, I have learned so much about myself. I am loved, I am usable regardless of my condition. I'm compassionate, unique and so much more. More and more layers of who I am to be are being laid upon me and transforming me. I am seeing the light of Christ in my life and seeing how I have a light to shine for others to see.

Now let's move on to more depth about the "in-between" of getting from a simple form to a precious pearl. After the form in the oyster accepts the grain of sand as part of its life, the oyster secretes layers upon layers of transparent material around the impure grain. Over time, it forms a shell. This shell is called nacre. Once the nacre has formed, it has accumulated character and a luster and becomes a beautiful pearl.

The more nacre it has, the greater the luminosity and the stronger the pearl. The luster is the brightness shining through from the pearl's inner core. My trials and lessons were forming a nacre over my life. I was and am building character and so much more.

"I am the light of the world" (John 8:12 NIV). God is the brightest light. He is the one with the greatest luster! Of all the characteristics of a pearl, luster is considered the most important, mostly because it is seen shining brilliantly from such a far distance. The luster of a pearl is rooted deep in the core. The greater the luster, the longer the pearl took to form. "'Do not consider his appearance or his height, for I have rejected him. The Lord does not look at the things people look at. People look at the outward appearance, but the Lord looks at the heart'" (1 Samuel 16:7 NIV) Its radiance causes the pearl to shine when the light shines within it. Christ is our light; He makes us shine when He is in our inner being. Our brightness to shine into a dying world could very well be our most life-giving characteristic. We cannot label people based on their appearance. Only God can know people's, inner heart.

Have you ever lost an item under a couch or bed? You get down on your hands and knees and squint until you find it. You cannot see anything. Finally, you get a flashlight and point it ahead. What happens? The darkness disappears! Not only do you find what you're looking for, but you might find a different item you probably didn't even know was missing. God's Word is our flashlight. With the Word, you can see where you are going and see what is missing in your life. Christ is our beacon; He shows us the direction to go. He helps us find what we are looking for. Sometimes, we might even see a verse in Scripture that we didn't know we were looking for, yet it got our attention. We also are the light for others. Our lives shine to show others the way, to show them what is missing in their lives.

The depth of nacre that forms the pearl luster depends on how long the intruding grain is left inside before it is formed. As the layers of nacre increase, so does the quality and durability of the pearl. As believers, the longer we are faced with our grains and the more we overcome, the stronger we become. We become rooted in the oyster for so long that when we are set free, we are strong because we have been immersed in Him.

Once the pearl's luster has formed, it immediately becomes a lantern that shines in the world. Everything that gets put in our path adds to our luster and the nacre strengthening us and making us brighter. Our outer strength is a witness to others, as well as our inner core. "I can do all this through Christ who gives me strength" (Phil 4:13 NIV). If we never had an irritant or sand in our lives, we would never evolve into becoming more like Him. We would never gain strength and a brighter luster. We would stay as a simple form in the darkness and never become that pearl.

This nacre shell, though hard, is not a layer that causes us to become cold and hard in a negative way. It makes us transparent and luminous so others can see Him in us. If you look closely enough at a genuine pearl, you see your own reflection. You are radiant and beautiful! Allow your radiance to reflect the light of Christ for all to see. We must be transparent so the crooked and perverse world will see Christ in us. Christ shines in us as we minister to others and care for them. Let us reflect Him in our luster. "God is light; in Him there is no darkness at all" (1 John 1:5 NIV)

Satan can disguise himself and pretend to be a light. He fools us into believing he is a genuine pearl. He can pretend to be a pearl or an angel of light, however, he cannot have our inner light core that shines strong. Satan can glimmer dimly, but only Jesus Christ shines bright enough to pierce to the core and be everlasting! "And no wonder, for Satan himself masquerades as an angel of light" (2 Cor. 11:14 NIV). Jesus is the morning star (Rev. 22:16). "But if we walk in the light, as He is in the light, we have fellowship with one another, and the blood of Jesus, His Son purifies us from all sin" (1 John 1:7 NIV) When John encountered false teachings, he illuminated the false and showed them the truth. Sometimes, the world is unable to make a distinction between fake and authentic pearl luster. There are some amazing "fakes" in our world. How can you tell a fake from a real one? Most of the time, you can tell by the depth of the luster without the pearl having to put forth any effort. It's not our job to judge and decide whether or not a person is a "fake" Christian. The fruit of a true believer will be marked by their behavior, words, and attitude. You will see the light of Christ in their lives.

What about fake pearls? The more a pearl reflects light, the greater its ability to draw the world in. A fake pearl does not reflect as much light, so it loses its ability to show Christ to the world. A hidden light is the same as one that reflects no light at all. "So that you may become blameless and pure, children of God without fault in a warped and crooked generation" (Phil 2:15 NIV) Don't hide your brilliance.

"Blessed is the one who perseveres under trial because, having stood the test, that person will receive the crown of life that the Lord has promised to those who love Him" (James1:12 NIV). Not only is the transformed pearl transparent and stronger. but also, it has formed depth and character. We, too, become stronger after facing our storms and calm seas. We are not thin and flimsy. Counterfeit pearls are thin and flimsy. We are people of strength, depth, and character. The more challenges we endure, the thicker our layers and our strength, the greater our endurance. "Be strong in the Lord and in His mighty power" (Eph. 6:10 NIV). We, too, reflect our testimony and all that goes along with the love of Christ. We reflect the working of the Holy Spirit. Carry your light-giving message into the dark!

The pearl's translucent luster not only reflects the light of Christ but also our joy. The Bible tells of laughter being the best medicine. "A cheerful heart is good medicine" (Prov. 17:22 NIV) While laughter is enjoyable and healing, laughter causes happiness, and happiness is based on our circumstances. Joy, on the other hand, is a deep, inner characteristic that reflects just as brightly as Christ. It goes to the depths of our being. If we have the joy of Christ, we are reflecting Him. Laughter is a great emotion; however, joy is even greater. Joy is a magnet that will draw others to you. Joy is also part of our strength. "Do not grieve, for the joy of the LORD is your strength" (Neh. 8:10b NIV).

"For you were once darkness, but now you are light in the Lord. Live as children of light...and find out what pleases the Lord" (Eph. 5:8-11 NIV). People in the dark are looking for direction to follow and be lead into the light.

"Your beauty should not come from outward adornments, such as elaborate hairstyles and the wearing of gold jewelry or fine clothes. Rather, it should be that of your inner self, the unfading beauty of a gentle and quiet spirit, which is of great worth in God's sight" (I Peter 3:3-4 ESV). Even though pearls have luster, they are not known for "stealing the show." That is not their goal. They are "attention getters" without even trying. Their goal is not to grab attention for selfish reasons, it is a natural part of who they are. Pearls don't cause us to focus on their outer appearance, but to look to their inner core. Their glow draws us in. As believers, our focus should not be on us, but on minimizing the focus on us and maximizing the focus on Him. We are not called to be "attention-getters" for our own satisfaction; we are called so others may see Him in us as part of our natural transforming image. We are not to exalt ourselves by drawing attention to ourselves. "For all those who exalt themselves will be humbled" (Luke 14:11 NIV). If you are a lighthouse, you don't need to blow your horn, just be a shining beacon.

Acknowledge that God is responsible for our achievements and our ability to be shining lights. Our testimony and our acts of service should be the "attention getters." He is working in our lives but not for selfish reasons or our outward appearance.

Acknowledging God lets others know to whom we give the credit. We also have internal peace and conviction of our beliefs and the world is drawn to them without them putting forth much effort. People watch our lives regardless of our drawing attention to ourselves or not. What message are you sending to the world? What is your light illuminating? What is your inner core saying? Is it louder than your outward appearance?

With diamonds, we tend to look at the stone's outer beauty. They sparkle and shine in such appealing ways. Most of us are drawn to a diamond's beauty yet it is also used as a distraction. That glitz and sparkle draw us in. Pearls, on the other hand, enhance the beauty of the owner and not of the object itself. "Do not consider his appearance...the Lord looks at the heart," (I Sam. 16:7 NIV).

There is a modern-day parable of candles shining their light. A man goes into his closet trying to find candles to light. The candles begin talking to him. One asks not to be taken out because he is not ready to be a light. Another candle says he is untrained and is doing research on being a candle. A third candle is enlightening on the importance of being a candle. And the last candle says he is waiting to get his act together before he will come out.

What are our excuses for not reflecting Christ? Are we not ready to be a light? He created us and embedded in us everything we require to fulfill His purpose. So how are we not ready? He commands us in His Word to go into the world and spread the light of Christ. "In the same way, let your light shine before others" (Matt 5:16a NIV). Is it because maybe the world seems like too big a place to start? So, be a light to one other person, or in your church, or your neighborhood. I guarantee there is someone else somewhere (probably close by) in the dark, who is needing your light to help guide them.

Are we untrained and prefer to do more research? If we are untrained, whose fault is it? Whose job is it to pray, read the word, attend church, grow, and be trained? Who requires you to do research? Studying and research are profitable for our spiritual well-being, although research only *informs* you. The Bible and God are the only ones who can *transform* you. "The heart of the discerning acquires knowledge, for the ears of the wise seek it out" (Prov. 18:15 ESV). Most at times, every bit of research and answer we need are in His Word. Our only requirement is to read it, study it, learn from it, store it in our hearts, and move on. "All Scripture is God-breathed and is useful for teaching, for rebuking, correcting, and for training in righteous- ness" (2 Tim. 3:16 NIV).

Must we really know the importance of being a can- dle? We are already chosen by Him so we already know we are important. Let Him bring you from the darkness into the light to be used. The greatest attrib- ute of light is it takes the darkness away.

Waiting to get your life in order? Which one of us can say our life is in perfect order so we can respond when God calls? Nobody has a perfect life. God doesn't ask us to have our lives in order before we begin doing on earth what He asks of us. It's not about us and what we can do. It's about God's grace giving us the ability. "Whatever turns up, grab it and do it. And heartily!" (Eccles. 9:10 MSG). He only asks that we keep busy, be available, and be willing to do whatever He asks. Be committed to Him. "Commit to the Lord whatever you do, and He will establish your plans" (Prov. 16:3 NIV) Abraham, David, Jonah, and many others didn't have their lives together, yet they were willing and God used them. God said He would give them the ability to act upon whatever He asked, and they believed Him and acted on it. It was not necessarily right away, but eventually, they did act upon it. If you accepted Christ, your life is together enough. He will fill in where you are lacking. He will supply you the strength and ability to accomplish what He has asked you to do. Asking you to perform difficult tasks, requires you to have more faith and trust in Him.

If you are dragging on and not being ready, quit, get your courage up and step out with your light. Let the Lord shine through you from the inside out. Show the world you are a woman after God's own heart!

Every challenging season I face and endure adds another layer to my core strength. The more layers I have, the stronger I become. The stronger I become, the brighter my light becomes. As I endure, I gain layers. May our light reflect God's beautiful design and handiwork. May those around us be drawn to the light in our hearts and our servanthood and not our outside appearances.

Remember your testimony. Celebrate and share your testimony. Let your actions speak louder than your words and draw people to Him. People are ultimately changed by our actions and not by our beliefs in them. His light in us is what draws them to Him. Make no excuses for your delay in sharing Him with others. Be the lighthouse in someone else's storm. When I was in the dark, He lit my path and showed me the way.

"I can see clearly now." Ingrid Simmonds

Chapter 11

Testimony for a Family Legacy

Jesus answered, 'Even if I testify on my own behalf, my testimony is valid, for I know where I came from and where I am going.' **John 8:14a [NIV]**

I have told you these things, so that in me you may have peace. In this world you will have trouble. But take heart! I have overcome the world. **John 16:33 [NIV]**

My people, hear my teaching; ......we will not hide these truths from our children, we will tell the next generation the praiseworthy deeds of the Lord, His power and the wonders He has done. Then they would put their trust in God and would not forget His deeds but would keep His commands. **Psalm 4:1; 4: 7 [NLT]**

I have a story and even though it may seem boring and mundane to me, it does not to God. He helped write my story and His plan is for me to share it. I have experienced enough to share my story to benefit somebody else. Even if I don't think I handled my grains very well, it's okay; sometimes with that comes some wisdom someone might need. The purpose of the story or testimony is not what happened to you. The purpose is that your story matters. Your struggles or lack of struggles encourage people now and for generations to come.

The pearl has its story of transformation from simple grain to intricate pearl. If it were human, it could testify with words and actions, but as a pearl, its testimony is visual in its transformation to core beauty. Jesus says in John 8 that he has a testimony and emphasizes its validity. Valid means it has strength and truth. "Jesus told them, 'These claims are valid even though I make them about myself .... I am one witness, and my Father who sent me is the other'" (John 8:14,18 NLT).

Your story is valid. Trials, struggles, and victories, all have helped create our testimony and we know it as truth. It is our "grain and grit story." He has applied His truth to me in a unique and personal way that makes me who I am and makes my story unique. Jesus has a testimony and we have a testimony. Share those testimonies! Our testimony is the "fruit" of what we have become.

My story is my testimony. Your story is your testimony. Your testimony was written by God and you. Nobody can argue with your story. Each one of us has her own testimony of how we came to be who we are and how we got where we are today. It is our story of how we came to know God in a very real way. Every trial and celebration we go through produce fruit or a testimony. Every struggle is a new chapter in our story and has a message. We carry our message to the world whether it's on purpose or not. (Isaiah 43:10)

God has chosen or allowed what experiences each one of us will suffer, endure, and celebrate. Every experience in every person's life creates a totally different human being, a totally different precious pearl.

The irritating sand produces a different variation of pearl, just like our struggles produce a different one of each of us. The growing process and the way we respond also produce a different result in each of our lives.

Though each process in each one of us is strengthening us and growing us, more crucial is what He will use us for from this point forward, based on our past experiences. In hindsight, those experiences made me who I am today. Looking forward, my experience becomes a testimony to encourage you to be who He made you, because of your own experiences. Look forward to opportunities to testify!

I have shared a bit of my life testimony with you. My testimony is my journey of my God living in me, working in my life, and bringing glory to Himself through me. My unique life experiences and creation testimony molded me and transformed me into the more confident believer I am today. The storms that blew through my life left grains of sand that He and I turned into grit for the future. I didn't ask for the sand, yet it came anyway.

When I was going through cancer treatments, I certainly didn't enjoy it. I wanted to spit my sand out! I didn't want that chapter to be in my story or testimony. I had to explore that chapter anyway. The most helpful thing I tried to focus on was the treatment and doctors who were saving my life. After I completed treatments and was told I was cancer-free, I was welcomed to the 5+ year club to which not many women survivors belonged. I would not waste this sand. There was no going back to the person I was before. What I thought might be the end wasn't the end after all. God was faithful and showed me the way forward to a better and more robust "fruit" or pearl.

A couple of years after my first cancer, a close friend had her cancer return. She had helped me physically and emotionally through my battle with cancer and at that moment, I knew it was my turn to help and encourage her as she went through her treatments again. Another friend's mother was also diagnosed with cancer soon after that. Again, I helped this friend with daily activities and helped her to understand what her mother was experiencing.

I have emailed and talked to people I don't even know. Various people knew others going through similar situations and asked me to share my experience with them as an encouragement to start their fight. My grain had become part of my testimony and I helped several people add to their testimony. What a sense of peace to know my cancer was not a waste. God blessed me with a second and third chance at life and I was not going to waste it. I was going to make sure my life with Him mattered. I was going to show others how God uses all things for good! Even when our lives seem like they've been destroyed, God can make our lives useful and make them matter. He is faithful and always with us.

The Bible is full of testimonies of God working in people's lives. Our testimony is not about what we have said and done but about what God has said and done through us. Our testimony focuses on Christ and His call to us to repent, be baptized and go into the world to do His work. Our testimony shows us going from seed to fruitful vine, from tiny clump to pearl. Everyone in the Bible has a testimony, Moses, David, all the disciples, Paul, and so on.

David's life and story have enough detail that we easily see his testimony. In 1 Samuel and Chronicles, David's life shows he was called by God as a child. His purpose didn't come to pass until He was anointed later in life. His whole life has been recorded so we can read of his testimony, the good fruit and the bad. Jabez probably has the shortest testimony, but powerful in its own way.

God gave David a hope and a future and he clung to that. He had days of being thrown around in storms, and days of smooth waves carrying him along. He brought some storms upon himself; he didn't always do what was right or what God desired for him. Even when he sinned though, he endured the consequences. When God forgave him, it did not take away the consequences of his sin *and* God still used him. He had plans for David's life. When David made the right choices by asking for forgiveness and changing, he was back on God's path for his life. Eventually, his son still died as a consequence of David's sin. Later, David could testify of the times when his heart wasn't right with God and the victorious times when He asked God FIRST what to do and then acted. When he received forgiveness for his sins, God restored him to a right relationship with Him. His story of forgiveness and reconciliation is an example to us; the more we experience that, the more we desire to tell others. Thousands of years later, we read of David's testimony and are encouraged by it.

The awesome part of having a testimony is we can share it with others to encourage them to allow God to continue to work in them. You may think you have arrived at being a complete person when life is terrific and your faith is strong but hold on! He isn't finished with your life or your testimony. It doesn't yet compare to the final result of who we will be on that final day. We must never stop changing. We never stop living and reaching for our future until we are home with Him. Each day we look back in hindsight and see pivotal moments when life didn't go as well because *we* were in control, not God. We also see pivotal moments when we allowed God to be in control and see how successful and how blessed we are as a result. God desires to transform us and make the successes greater than the failures.

Most testimonies will become generational. We have one such testimony in our family. It was written down and has been told for generations by word-of-mouth. It still inspires us today. My husband had a great-great-grandfather seven generations back who served the Lord. He was shipwrecked and left on a rock in the ocean. He told the Lord if He rescued him to live another year, he would serve Him forever and he proceeded to sit on the rock and sing praises at the top of his lungs for many days. He was eventually rescued and served the Lord and had revivals on his land for another 20 years. We love to read the story even today. This man believed in the power of God and entrusted himself and his family to God's care for generations. He was faithful to God. When you share that kind of testimony with someone, it has a powerful ripple effect. The word-of-mouth testimony travels on and on and farther and farther out.

Rejoice in your testimony! Rejoice in your sufferings and sand and learn from them. Turn them into your grit and testimony. Don't waste a single grain. Use it all for Him. "Not only that, but we rejoice in our

sufferings, knowing that suffering produces endurance, and endurance produces character, and character produces hope, and hope does not put us to shame,
because God's love has been poured into our hearts
through the Holy Spirit who has been given to us"
(Rom. 3:3-5 NIV).

Even if you have never walked through difficult
times, you still have a testimony. Your testimony is
that you have been spared from the worst of adversities in life. Your testimony is not how "bad" you were;
it's who God has been in your life up to that point. It's
about how your life matters and God working in your
life is evidence or fruit of that. Your story might be as
calm and simple as God loves you, died for you, and
you chose to live for Him and will obtain eternal life.
On the other hand, many believers have many stories
and a long, crazy, radical testimony of everything they
have accomplished or endured.

Being a Christian doesn't change what diseases
we get, what adversities we endure, or what struggles
we face. It doesn't change all the obstacles in our
path. It just means we have God with us always; it
changes how we handle them. We are not the focus or
main character in the story, Jesus is!

So, what's the difference between a story and testimony? A story is a narrative of your life and past
events. Sometimes, our "story" is as short as who we
are, where we came from and where we are headed.
Many times, there are a great number of chapters in a
person's life. Sometimes it is passed down by word-of-
mouth or sometimes it is written down. Everyone has
a story.

A testimony is a solid declaration proving God is

who He says He is, whether it is spoken or read. It is an awesome account of the Holy Spirit being in control of your life and working through you in all circumstances. It proves God's love and saving grace as people see His power working in you. "And this is the testimony, that God gave us eternal life, and this life is in his Son" (1 John 5:11 NIV)

My story, in a nutshell, is I grew up in an average, middle-class home, with a good, solid family. My father was in the Army and my mother was a housewife. We always attended church. My father was sent to Vietnam and my mother sent the four of us children to Vacation Bible School (VBS) for her sanity. I accepted Christ as my Savior on the last day of VBS. I finished high school and went to college. I graduated from college. I married and had three children. Life was easy and comfortable. Then came cancer. I fought it twice and I am still here living and breathing.

My testimony is so much more. I can show you instance after instance of God's presence giving me peace and reminding me, He is in control. I can show you how God continues to use me. I can show you fruit from my trials. Now my life has more grace, character, fruit, and humility, stronger faith, strength, endurance...... My declaration is: God is who He says He is. Circumstances and struggles may change but my God never changes!

He was with me in the waters. I got wet but they didn't flow over me. He was with me in the fire. Things got hot but I didn't burn. My story is a powerful testimony of the living, breathing God. It shows what adversities and victories He has brought me through, and hopefully, it encourages others to swim through the tides of life and endure being wet up to their necks.

Revelation 12:11 says we can overcome the enemy by the power of our testimony. When you share your testimony to help someone see their testimony, then what you call your "burden" becomes a jewel of beauty for all to see. There is power in my testimony. There is power in your testimony!

"For I consider that the sufferings of this present time are not worth comparing with the glory that is to be revealed in us" (Romans 8:18 NIV). Everyone has storms that invade their lives, those storms leave grains of sand and grit. Even though it seems an enormous amount of sand is blocking your vision, it is neither as big as it appears nor as big as your blessing on the other side. But sometimes, the worst outcome will still happen. You won't call it a victory. Even though it is hard and you don't want to say it, the fact is, God is still God and He is still there. He is still with you. At some point, you will be able to dig through your pain and find a blessing. And, when you find that blessing, you will have a testimony to share!

When Peter and Paul were in jail, it was probably the worst outcome in their minds, yet they had no clue there would be an earthquake. The quake of destruction was their rescue. God rescued them and they thanked Him and worshiped Him. In 2 Chronicle, when Jehoshaphat led Judah into battle, he appointed men to sing to the Lord and praise Him. As they began to sing, God set ambushes against the enemy. They still had to fight and face whatever darkness came their way, but in their praising Him during darkness came their rescue and testimony. What a testimony of God's faithfulness to their obedience they had to share then!

When the grains of sand get embedded in our lives, we have a choice to make. We can try and spit the sand out or accept it, pray through it, and allow the Holy Spirit to make it a part of our testimony. We can also choose to remain a simple form for the rest of our lives and not allow transformation. Every grain we refuse to take, we surrender to the enemy. Don't let the enemy have anything!

Find opportunities to share your testimony. Your testimony and scars are evidence you were almost destroyed or broken, slowly repaired, but you are still fully functional and you are the fruit of His vine. As long as you have breath, you have a job to do.

Ultimately, my testimony goes back to when I was born. It gets really fulfilling when I accepted Christ as my Savior up to today. It means I have 40 years' worth of trudging or dancing through situations and circumstances and wading through sand, knowing God more and more. My life started as a story and now it has been changed into a testimony of the love, grace, mercy, and faithfulness of God. I have a testimony of being broken and restored. God uses our lives as testimonies of His goodness, grace, and mercy. People need to know they are not the only ones working through waves of the terrific and the disastrous.

Don't hide your testimony. Your testimony is your treasure to someone else. Your testimony does not end when you become a Christian. Your story continues to be written. Even with all my years of experiences, my testimony is still being created with God's covering over me. Every decision you make, every action, every attitude, and the way you react are all part of your story for others to hear and see. "But as for you, continue in what you have learned and have firmly believed, knowing from whom you learned it and how from childhood you have been acquainted with the sacred writings, which are able to make you wise for salvation through faith in Christ Jesus" (2 Tim. 3:14-15 ESV). Though times have changed from David in the Old Testament, God is still in our story. Every story is different but the Author of Life is the same. God is still in control. He is still the testimony of our living hope and future.

Think about what story you want to be able to tell in the future. Do you want a story like David who was anointed, a man after God's heart, was successful and used by God? Let Him be in control; He will work in you and through you. He will do for you what He did for David. He will write you an awesome testimony.

I discovered in this next layer for me that I have wisdom and experiences to share and encourage others. My testimony or story is important to somebody. Somebody's ear is waiting to hear about God's power and His working in my life. And it is fine if others don't want to hear your story. Not everyone will be ready to hear it when you are ready to tell it. They may never want to hear it and that's okay.

Think how far you have come as a Christian. He will bring you through more. You might get wet but you won't drown. You might get hot but you won't burn. It's not about getting wet or getting hot, it's about who's in the flood and fire with you. God is at work in our wet storms and hot fires, even when we can't see it. We can't see the wind but we know it's there. We can't see God but we must believe He is there. He will reach down at any moment, and with one touch of His hand, He will change an impossible situation in your life. Regardless of whether your story has a "supernatural" aspect, it is still a story of the great works of our

God.

Whatever testimony or story you leave is your legacy. Make sure your legacy is a Godly legacy. My pilgrimage also has a final, everlasting destination. I have a story on my way to that destination. My story is my legacy. I have a legacy for my children and grandchildren. "Behold, children are a heritage from the Lord" (Psalm 127:3 NIV).

It's not so important as to how well I handled my life, what matters is that I let God work in, and on that final day His work will be complete. Regardless of whether your story has miracles of our God or not, there is evidence of Him and whatever proof you leave is your legacy. As I said, make sure your legacy is a Godly legacy. Whatever story you tell to the future is your legacy.

A pearl's creation is not wasted on staying simple. Their grains have been used to show God's power in each of the stories we will pass on to future generations. What story do you want to show future generations?

"Find your purpose in your trials." Ingrid Simmonds

Chapter 12

Your Faith and the Power of Prayers

Jesus said to them, 'Truly, I tell you, if you have faith and do not doubt, not only can you do what was done to the fig tree, but also you can say to this mountain, "Go, throw yourself into the sea," it will be done. If you believe, you will receive whatever you ask for in prayer.' **Matt. 21:21-22 [NIV]**

Again, I believed my faith was strong before cancer, but I was mistaken. It's easy to have a strong faith when everything is just rolling along so well. Cancer didn't cause me to doubt my faith, it forced me to turn my grains into a new layer in my faith. I turned them into a lesson learned. Grains are not a curse. They are an opportunity to strengthen our faith. Our faith is also not based upon circumstances; seeing our way through hard times does strengthen us if we let it.

"Now faith is the assurance of things hoped for and the conviction of things not seen" (Heb. 11:1 NIV). Faith is complete trust in God. It is trusting Him because of His Word and authority without further evidence. It's believing He is who He says He is. It's about believing He will do what He says He will do. My faith is also based on past experiences of Him working in my life, so I anticipate Him even more in the future.

During my bouts with cancer (and any other trials in my life), what meant more to me than anything was knowing people were praying for me daily. I had always prayed over the years, but this newly-found peace and comfort in knowing others were praying for me was special. Because I found such comfort and strength in that, I began to pray more earnestly for others needing prayer; that is a simple yet impactful way to help and encourage others.

At times, we all feel like our faith and prayer life are in a desert. It feels like you are parched, dry and stagnant. It feels like you are just going through the motions. I know we've all been there. Can't find the words? Sometimes one earnest word from you is all it takes to find an answer.

You might need restoration in your relationship with Him. You might need the joy of your salvation restored to you. It's so much easier to talk to someone when your relationship is right. If you keep your relationship with God right, then He's so much easier to talk to. "Then you will call upon me and come and pray to me, and I will hear you" (Jer. 29:12 NIV).

I was at a rough, low period several years ago. It wasn't that I lost my faith, I lost my focus and, ultimately, I lost my joy too. I had so many things that seemed stacked against me. It was after I started pulling away from others and my church that life became more difficult. I was so focused on me and "feeling good" and "being happy" that I lost my real purpose and my focus on Him. My eyes were wandering. I knew it was my own doing, but I didn't know how to get back on track and find that inner joy again.

We were visiting a church one Sunday and they asked people to come forward if they wanted prayer. I went forward (which was a miracle for me). I never go forward and ask for prayer, but I was desperate. The elders laid hands on me and prayed for me. They didn't know what my prayer request was. In my heart, I asked God to take me back where we started and restore the joy of His salvation to me. They prayed over my unknown request. I went back to my seat and the service went on. As we were leaving, I went over to the pastor to shake hands and tell him how much I enjoyed the service. When he took hold of my hand, I felt a very warm, electricity flow through me in an unusual manner.

We got into the car to head home, and before we had left the parking lot, I had begun laughing hysterically in the back seat. My daughter had her learner's permit so she was driving and my husband rode up-front with her. She wanted to know if anything was wrong with her driving. "Nothing!" I said laughing. I continued to laugh. I laughed all the way home. That same afternoon, I was paying bills and just began laughing. Throughout the week, at unusual times, I would burst out laughing, never at a time or place that would embarrass me. There was such joy in my laughter. I realized, after a couple of days, that God had literally restored the joy of my salvation to me. I was ecstatic.

The joy was not because pain and turmoil in my life had stopped but He had returned me to my spiritual beginning and a fresh start. The difficult things in my life were still there, yet the joy was a reminder and confidence-builder that despite my struggles, He was still there with me and will always be. He is still there even in my sorrows and dry seasons. Never doubt God if your faith is struggling and your path is unclear, dry, sorrowful, and full of obstacles. There is hope for new joy. Sometimes all you need to do is ask Him. "Restore to me the joy of your salvation and uphold me a willing spirit" (Psalm 51:12 NIV). As the Message version of the Bible says, "Put a fresh wind in my sails".

I realize not everyone will have such a quick answer to their prayers. I don't know why some prayers don't seem to be answered. I just leave it all in God's hands anyway. It never hurts to pray and ask Him. The point of my story is to show you that all you need to do is ask. He will answer your prayer in whatever way He chooses, but He *does* hear you. If I hadn't still had a smidgeon of faith, I would not have prayed, but I had just enough. If we did not have faith in Him, we would not pray.

Even if you are not a believer and pray as a last resort, He may still hear and answer your prayer. Many Muslim believers are having prayers answered and hearing from God even when they don't believe in Him. We must have faith to pray and we must pray in faith.

"Pray without ceasing" (I Thess. 5:17 ESV). What is prayer? Prayer is our privilege to communicate with God. We cannot be on our knees all the time; nevertheless, we can have a prayerful attitude in our thoughts, words, and actions. It can be simple prayers throughout your day, like when I hear and see an ambulance go by, I say a prayer for the person who is or will be in it. When I hear of a missing person report, I say a quick prayer that the person will be found. You can pray all day without ceasing. Make Him the person you speak to first thing every morning before you talk to anyone else. We are usually anxious to speak to Him but are we anxious to hear back from Him? If we will wait and listen, He speaks back to us. Pray in thoughts, words, and actions, that is without ceasing.

"Continue steadfastly in prayer" (Col. 4:2 NIV.) Start every day with prayer. Prayers are not to be the last resort that you think of after you're already in trouble or after you have tried to work out a situation on your own. If you only pray when you are in trouble, your relationship is in BIG trouble. Pray before you do anything; pray in everything; praise Him when you're crossing that river. Pray constantly about people and/or situations.

"God has surely listened and heard my prayer" (Psalm 66:19 NIV). Be persistent in your prayers. Persistence does not mean to pray in endless repetition. It requires us to pray for a need, request, or over others, for a while. Even if your answers come slowly, remember He hears you; the delay might be what is best for you or the other person involved. His answer to your prayer might be wiser than your request was. Prayer is not always about "getting your way;" sometimes, it's about changing you, not your situation. When you get an answer, thank Him, because you know He surely listened and heard your prayer.

Anything you do, anywhere you go, and anything you say without praying first, says to God, "I know what I'm doing. I can handle this myself on my own strength. I don't need You." And then you probably fall flat on your face!

The best time to get help for how, what, and when,

or for direction when you are at a crossroads in life, is to have prayed yesterday, so when you get to that point, you already have an idea of the answer or decisions could be clearer. If you didn't pray about it yesterday, it's never too late to start. Start to pray today. Even your last breath is not too late to take time to pray.

Keep your eyes on God when you pray and not on the "happening" that got you to pray in the first place. I learned this through a very "hands-on" experience. Years ago, I was on a mission trip to Mexico. I woke up in the middle of the night with the worst stomach pain I had ever experienced. I went into the bathroom to see if I could empty my bowels (sorry, but that was the truth), but nothing happened and the pain only grew worse. I was sharing a hotel room with three other women. I woke them up and told them about my pain. They laid hands on me and prayed and nothing happened. The whole time they were praying, I was letting them pray and focusing on how much it hurt. When they finished, I realized it was important for me to participate and worship as though He had already heard my prayers.

The focus should be to worship Him, not to feel better. Worship Him because He is God! I asked the women to pray again. I immediately began focusing on God and who He is. I was worshiping Him with my heart and thanking Him that He heals. I began to feel my body grow very warm. The warmth inside started at my feet, worked its way up through my body, and out of my head. As it went, the warmth took all of the pain with it. When we stopped praying, the pain was completely gone. To this day, I have *never* had that same pain again. Your focus and heartful attitude make a big difference in your prayers. Prayer is speaking words, focus, and worship.

God understands the prayers of our heart, even if we can't find the words to utter them, or if the words you do find seem insufficient. Many days during chemo, I was so overwhelmed emotionally that I could not find words to say. Sometimes, it's just best to sit, be still, and listen without words. Let Him do the talking to your heart. Sometimes, your tears of pain or joy are enough of prayer to His ears. Try finding a word or phrase and say it over and over again, letting it sink into your spirit. In Matthew 14:30, Peter prayed a quick, to-the-point prayer, "Lord, save me!" Sometimes, that's all it takes. His Word never comes back void. "Likewise, the Spirit helps us in our weakness. We do not know what to pray for as we ought, but the Spirit himself intercedes for us with groanings too deep for words." (Rom. 8:26) [NIV]

I remember during Bible studies when the leader would ask for prayer request, I would never utter a prayer request. None of my requests ever seemed "big enough" or important enough to have others pray about them. They seemed minuscule, in light of others' requests. I have come to learn, if my request is a burden to me and weighing me down, then it is a burden to God. "Any concern too small to be turned into a prayer is too small to be made into a burden."[3] He cares about every little detail in our life.

If you pray and tell God you're laying everything down at His feet, but instead of turning around and

---

[3] Ten Boom, Corrie (2020). https://www.brainyquote.com/quotes/corrie_ten_boom_135077. Brainy Media, Inc.

walking away from it, you back away, keeping your eyes on what you laid down, then you haven't laid it down. Hannah in 1 Samuel was effective and fervent in worship and prayer. She believed God for a son. In faith, she gave Samuel back to God and devoted her life to Him anyway. She knew how to lay things down. The way I lay things down is to pour out my prayer and my feelings to Him on my knees with my face to the floor, I pray until I have said all I can, and it feels lifted to me then.

How about a distracted prayer or half focused prayer? Have you ever tried to pray and the things you are trying to keep out of your mind while you pray, keep popping up anyway? Have you ever told a child to do something while they continued playing? You don't have their full attention. They say, "uh huh," and whatever you asked them to do isn't done. It's the same when we're praying. God desires your *full attention*. God wants you to look Him in the face (spiritually speaking), ask with your whole heart, *and* listen to what He is saying to you. He needs your focus and attention on Him, not your "uh huh."

Your biggest distraction might be that you are listening with a reply ready, instead of listening to understand what He is saying. One way I found to get rid of my distraction was to pray about whatever came to mind and then it was no longer there. Sometimes, if you pray with a family member or friend, it's harder to get distracted. I also play worship music and get my mind back into His presence. Pray by starting with reading Scripture out loud.

Even the disciples in the garden struggled with prayer. We all struggle, yet God knows our hearts and mind. He understands our humanness. Just go to Him with an open heart and find what keeps you focused on Him. Persist in a prayer time with Him. "And He told them a parable to the effect that they ought always to pray and not lose heart." (Luke 18:1) [NIV]

My favorite kind of prayer is usually when I have hit an all-time low (sometimes I start with this kind of prayer). It's a prayer of submission or relinquishment. I physically get down with my face on the floor and just begin to worship Him. My desire is to be brought to a place physically, as well as emotionally and spiritually, where I can hear God and be profoundly changed. I am in His presence. In Daniel 6, Daniel prays three times a day on his knees, just giving thanks to God. At times, I don't pray for anything specific; I just worship Him and surrender all my emotions to Him. I give Him my full focus and attention. I figure the way <u>up</u> to Him is to be <u>down</u> on my face and knees.

Prayer is not always praying for yourself. When you are aware others are hurting or going through a difficult time, pray for them even if they don't ask. If someone asks you to pray for them, by all means, PRAY! If you don't intend on praying for someone, please don't say you will. There are times we will honestly just forget to pray and that's okay. Sometimes people would say to me, "I'll pray for you." It came across as trite because I knew they weren't believers. When I put updates on my Facebook page, many people would put up the praying hands emoji, and I wondered how many would really pray for me, or if that was just an easy way for them to handle a tough situation. I'm guilty of the same thing. Maybe it's not important to some, but to me, it made a world of difference to know others really were praying for me. Does it matter if 50 people are praying for you or one person is praying? James says pray for one another and the prayers of <u>a</u> righteous man, that is, *one* righteous man, have great power. I don't know the answer, but I still felt better knowing more than one person was praying for me. One person praying brings more than nobody. I believe prayer is one of the reasons I am still here. As warriors, it is our job to pray for one another, especially if someone specifically asks us to pray. If you think you might forget, offer to pray, then and there.

Without faith and prayer, where would we be? (Matthew 21:21-22) There are many unanswered questions in life which make our faith and prayer necessary. I could face tomorrow with my trials because of my prayers and the prayers of others for me. There is power in prayer. With prayer, we can face anything in life because of our faith in Him. When my prayer was just words, He gave me a heart for Him. He rewards those who seek Him.

"Life's roughest storms prove the strength of our anchor." Ingrid Simmonds

Chapter 13

Oysters Still Speak

All scripture is breathed out by God and is profitable for teaching, for reproof, for correction and for training in righteousness that the man of God may be complete, equipped for every good work. **Tim. 3:16-17 [NIV]**

Let me hear what God the Lord will speak, for He will speak peace to His people, to His saints. **Psalm 85:8 [NLT]**

I knew early on in my Christian walk that God willingly speaks and responds to us. It was a deep, inner confidence I'd had since I was a child. It has never been audible, but at times, it seems so. I really hadn't heard Him speak much to me over the years, because I didn't know how to listen and I didn't recognize His voice yet. Through stressful difficult seasons in my life, the choice that seemed clear to me was to seek Him more diligently than I ever had before. I spent hours reading His Word, listening to sermons, doing Bible studies, reading books on the Christian life, and praying. The result was, I knew His character and now recognized when He was speaking to me. The more I prayed, worshiped, and studied, the more He revealed insights and direction to me and spoke to my heart.

God does still speak to us today. Even in our struggles, He is there. God speaks to us, the same God who created us, the galaxies, and all of creation chooses to speak to us. He speaks to us through His Word, through other believers, through His Spirit, through worship, through prayer, and through circumstances. And yes, He does know who He's talking to. He chooses to speak to you specifically. He doesn't just speak to people in the Bible. We know He did speak to them, He never changes, so He will still speak to us today. "Jesus Christ is the same yesterday, and today and forever" (Heb. 13:8 NIV). Whatever and however He speaks to us, if it is Him, it will line up with His Word. Nothing will contradict His Word or His character.

The more time you spend with God in His Word, devotions, studying Him, and being in His presence, the more you come to know His character, and the more you will recognize His voice when He speaks to you. If you get angry with Him and quit speaking to Him, you will forget what His voice sounds like.

You always remember the presence of God and what He speaks to you even years later. I remember dreams vividly from 40 years ago when I felt God speaking to me. I can tell you every little detail to this day. He tends to speak to me in dreams. "I will pour out my Spirit on all people .... your old men shall dream dreams, and your young men shall see visions.... In those days I will pour out my Spirit" (Joel 2:28 NIV). He does still speak to us in dreams.

"You make known to me the path of life; in your presence there is fullness of joy; at your right-hand pleasures forevermore" (Psalm 16:11 NKJV). There is life and joy in His presence. The times you have been

and are in God's presence help shape you into the believer you are today. You will look back on those times
when you are in a season of not knowing where God
is, or if He is hearing you. Remember He *does* hear you
and will speak to you again.

I have experienced Him speaking to my heart many
times. At times, when reading His Word, a phrase will
get my attention or jump out at me. Sometimes, I get a
sentence about what the selection of Scripture is to
me. I believe those to be God speaking to me specifically for my specific needs and circumstances. Somebody else could read the same Scripture and get a message from it that seems specifically fit for them. Sometimes, a Scripture speaks to you to which others would
say, "That is not what it is saying or referring to."
Maybe not to them, but the Word was for me, something specific to my needs that I had to hear or know.
And you can read a Scripture many times and get nothing from it, then one day, it speaks to you like never
before.

Three years ago, we believed we were to move to
Florida. We had a plan in mind that we believed God
had given to us that would come to fruition. We lived
in New Mexico at the time and had for 40 years. We
had a son in Wisconsin, a son in Texas, and a daughter
in Ohio. Not too far, yet far enough to not get to visit
often. Florida fell apart for reasons we could see only
being from God. Our middle son asked us to consider
moving to Texas to be near two of our five grandchildren. Things began to fall into place and we ended up
in Texas. We love our new home, neighborhood, and
church, but a part of me was still whining about not
moving to Florida.

I was whining to God one day and asked Him why

He didn't follow through on "our plan." Clearly, in my heart, (not audibly) a voice said, "Go back and look at the Scripture I gave you for your life." I had always focused on Isaiah 43: 1-4 even though He had given me verses 1-12. This time, I looked at the next section. "Fear not, for I am with you; I will bring your descendants from the east (my daughter had moved from Ohio back to Texas), and gather you from the West (we moved from the west); I will say to the north, 'give them up!' (our son in Wisconsin moved south to Arizona) Bring my sons from afar, and My daughters from the ends of the earth."

That all may say nothing to anybody else but it was confirmation for us from God. He had impressed upon me way back in 2005 that I would be with my grandchildren and be a spiritual mentor to them., and it was happening, Two of our grandkids were here near us. Granted, Arizona is almost as far from us as Wisconsin was from NM, but it is miles closer to us now. The north gave them up to the south. He spoke specifically to our situation. These verses have been confirmed to me again and again.

His Word is active and more powerful than anything. Read and *listen* to His Words. "In the beginning was the Word, and the Word was with God, and the Word was God" (John 1:1 NIV). "For the word of God is living and active, sharper than any two-edged sword" (Heb. 4:12a NIV). The Word of God is our weapon. If we memorize Scripture, it is in our hearts and we can use that weapon anytime. That Word is speaking to us as long as we keep reading it.

Make it a habit to be thankful that we have the Word and have a healthy, reverence for His Word. Set your mind on things above and not earthly things. "For to set the mind on the flesh is death, but to set the mind on the Spirit is life and peace" (Romans 8:6 NIV). The Word of God is alive and when it is in your heart, it works! Consciously choose every day to center your focus and life on God and His Word. Study and memorize His Word.

Every morning after I read Scripture, I jot down in a journal what the Holy Spirit is saying to me. After that, I pray. Sometimes He shows me more that I feel must be written down. Sometimes it is as simple as re-writing one verse in my own words. Other days, I write quite a bit. Every once in a while, I go back and read previous entries to see how far I have come and what God has accomplished in my life. I reread my journal in the spring of 2014 just months after being diagnosed with cancer. I realized after reading my entries starting in November 2013, revelations and thoughts God had brought to my attention to write were showing me how He had gone before me regarding my cancer. He went ahead of me and was preparing me. I wrote things like: "If the plan He has for me seems un-doable, it isn't. He will work in and around me;" "Don't look at the size or 'impossibility' of a task. If He asks you to do it, He will see you through it;" "Remember in the dark times what He told you in the light;" also, "And with His wounds we are healed." I had copied down Isaiah 53:2, verses 4-7 (verses on healing) [NIV] and replaced the word "our" with my name. Why would I have written down all those verses? We've got to believe God speaks to us through many different avenues!

Others I run across now label me a "Survivor." I don't really like that term. To me, it says I outlived another trial by the skin of my teeth and now I am barely alive. If I must use a word to define me now, I would call myself a *thriver.* As a thriver or an overcomer, I have fought with God's help and have grown and changed. I have moved on to something better. So, now my question to Him is: "Who am I that You have brought me this far? Why do I deserve this grace and mercy?" Like David in 2 Samuel when he asks God, "Who am I, that you have brought me this far?" I humbly accept God's grace in my life.

I looked forward to being used even more by God. The fact that there is still breath in me tells me God will still use me here. He continues to speak to me about helping others with their struggles. I have an assignment here that is bigger than my wounds and the enemy.

I have redefined my past as a challenge that the grains I experienced were showing God was with me every step of the way. It was a challenge that we conquered together. He was the power behind my putting one step in front of the other all the way through this part of my journey. He was my strength when I was weak. He used that period of my life to teach me many things and I can use those lessons for future ministry to others. Survivors still have "wounds" that need healing.

Thrivers have healed wounds but have scars to show others how to be more than a survivor. I am an overcomer. Romans 8:37 declares we have been made MORE than conquerors. And, I am not here because I had surgery and treatments, I am here because of GOD'S GRACE. I don't deserve to be here more than anyone else, and I didn't earn it. I am here because of God's grace and the prayers of His people. I did my part and went to appointments and treatments and followed their suggestions for minimizing effects. I did my part and God's grace for me did the rest.

I came through as a "richer" person than when I went in. That is the way it is when you have God besides you. In Exodus 12, when God delivered His children, they didn't escape with nothing. When God delivered them, they picked those Egyptians clean and came out with all those riches. They had survived the battle but now they were richer. Ultimately, God desires more for us than to even thrive; He wants us to live in the abundance of His presence every day. Throughout that part of my journey, God did not listen to me more or speak to me more than when things were going well. He is always speaking. I just needed Him more, so I pressed in more to hear His voice.

None of this surviving and thriving or "getting through" would have happened if I had not tuned my heart and ears to hear His voice. God spoke to Moses more than once in the Old Testament: "And there Moses received life-giving words to pass onto us" (Acts 7:38 NIV). God never changes. He still speaks to us today. He can give us live-giving words also.

Now that I have been free for 14 years from breast cancer and free 5+ years from ovarian cancer, I am at a crossroads. I stand here and pray about what's next. I won't stand and wait for the next load of sand. I will begin to move forward in faith to where I feel God is leading. It's a struggle for me because I feel I have been given a second *and* third chance at life. I must live life with even more purpose at this very moment! I feel a weight and responsibility, none the less, it is *not* a bad feeling. I'm still listening and moving forward.

This book really isn't to be focusing on the fact that

I had cancer. I want the focus to be on God and His power and all that He can do in and through us if we let Him. It's about how His goodness and grace work in our lives. It's about allowing the Holy Spirit to comfort and guide us. It's about not wasting trials and/or life experiences. It's about having been so profoundly changed by a challenging encounter so He could bring me to a place where I can hear Him better. He can bring you to a place of hearing Him also. Learning these lessons and about the character of God gives us relief on our journey from the burden of "jaw-dropping, gut-punching" circumstances. It closes our jaws a little and lets us breathe easier.

I know many others have endured much more and much harder than I, but it's all relative. God gives you whatever or however much you need to be drawn to Him and molded into His image. What is considered a challenging trial for me may not be for someone else. We are all different. It's about yours and His story, written through your life, how you are drawn to Him, and how He draws people to Him because of your testimony.

I am overwhelmingly grateful to the One who has spoken the deepest, clearest words to me in the darkest seasons of my life. My dearest, cherished treasure is the songs He places in my heart to worship and exalt Him to the highest place and those words defeat the enemy. JOY did come in the morning!

"God is about as silent as an ocean." Ingrid Simmonds

Chapter 14

Celebrate Life

This is the day the Lord has made. We will rejoice and be glad in it. **Psalm 118:24 [NIV]**

You will show me the way of life, granting me the joy of your presence and the pleasures of living with you forever. **Psalm 16:11 [NIV]**

For you make me glad by your deeds, O Lord; I sing for joy at the works of your hands. **Psalm 92:4 [NIV]**

As you can probably tell by now, each time, I learned a bit of wisdom from my adversities and battles, it was a new layer of His image that was added to me, making me a stronger, sturdier pearl. The more layers I have and learn from, the more pearl-like I become. Life is not about just continuing in the same state without having died, it's about thriving in expectation of God working in us to make us more like Him, because of what we have endured. It's prospering, flourishing, increasing in faith and sharing that "wealth." It's about making it worthwhile to pull through our struggles. It's about making our fruit the juiciest, the best, the most satisfying.

We are people who need spiritual transformation and restoration. He *wants* to transform our hearts and minds. He *wants* us to be restored to fulfill His plan that He originally had for us. He *doesn't want* us to just be saved and be transformed to be more like Him. We will reflect the glory and power of our God. He will restore us physically, as well as spiritually (Ezekiel 36:26).

God allows grains into our lives periodically. Sometimes the grains seem to mount up to the size of a mountain. Don't focus on the mountain of adversity. Shift your focus to the One who created the mountains. He chose you, planted you where you are, and takes care of you as if you were the only one. Find the beauty in your sometimes rocky path and through the obstacles, because you are priceless, cherished, irreplaceable, usable, and worth so much to God!

We are people of purpose and worth. We are each born with a life plan that was designed before we were born. Throughout life, we each acquire character and a testimony that God gives us to fulfill His purpose for us. We can build up other men and women, families, marriages, and the church body. We must not make excuses for *not* becoming all He has created us to be. We are important and valued.

Many years ago, I started a bowl of what I call memorial stones. I got the idea from reading Joshua Chapter 4. Every time God would bring us through something difficult or worth celebrating, I would write it on a rock with the date and put it in my bowl. It was my reminder (or journal of sorts) for when times were rough; it reminded me of all the things God already brought me through, battle or victory. Now, when people ask me, "What do these stones mean?" I can tell them. Now, we have grandchildren who have begun to ask me what each rock is. I am excited to tell them each story and they love finding the rock with their birth on it. I now have a rock I can write, in faith, "Pandemic 2020," because He WILL bring us through and His power and might WILL be shown! We will have this memory to testify all that He has done in this time. "These stones will stand as a memorial among the people of Israel forever" (Joshua 4:7 NLT).

As you create your story, learn to testify about it and share it with others. Testify and leave a legacy! Your faith is an example. Your example and your prayers cause others to follow in their own transformations. Regardless whether your story tells about the great works of our God, whatever you leave is a legacy. Make sure the legacy is a Godly legacy. Whatever story you tell to the future is about you and your God. When you withstand your grains and storms and trust God to bring the best outcome in your life, your actions provide a testimony of your grit, growth, and a legacy to leave for future generations. "We will not hide these truths from our children; we will tell the next generation about the glorious deeds of the Lord, His power, and the wonders He has done" (Psalm 78:4 NIV),

Continue in your prayer life. Leave time for God to speak to you. It is a two-sided relationship, not one way. "Watch and pray." Prayer is essential to keep our defenses up against the enemy. Let prayer be your natural response throughout your day. "The earnest prayer of a righteous person has great power and produces wonderful results" (James 5:16b NIV).

We are not the strong ones in life; we are just the shell God's power works through if we allow Him. Don't let the waves full of sand and the storms knock you over. He put those waves in front of us so we will rely on Him to stay standing when their stinging grains and powerful forces come again. Are you willing to step forward, even when you know that wave is bringing another grain of sand? "So, after you have suffered a little while, he will restore, support and strengthen you on a firm foundation" (I Peter 5:10 NKJV). We are to be pearls in the making.

I read articles and posts about "what I learned from cancer." I'm not sure if I would put it that way. Cancer has no redeeming value, but God can use it to bring something beautiful to our lives. He can use cancer to teach us. I did learn from God through cancer. I took many difficult tests and learned many life-changing valuable answers. Cancer caused me to face some of my fears and my own mortality. I have learned from my challenging life experiences and circumstances.

All that wisdom is great, but what I really learned was so much more about God's character and who He is. I learned that nothing difficult will silence my worship of God. Worship is part of my warfare. Worship Him, even when you don't feel like it because worship is the first blow to the enemy. I find joy, not in the absence of trials, but in the presence of God in situations and my worship. I declare His truths, even when I don't feel like it.

We, as believers who choose to become more like God, are people of excellence and ability, expected to carry out His plan for us with character, integrity, our life experiences, our lessons learned, our compassion, our prayers, faith, and our testimony. When Jesus asked the disciples to follow Him, they dropped what they were doing and immediately followed Him. They were available and chose to become more like Him. Our ability doesn't matter, as much as our "availability."

Becoming a pearl means you must let go of the sand after it causes you pain. Let Him heal you and leave a scar if He chooses. Even Jesus has scars and they don't tell a story of defeat. They are a sign of victory. Let your scars be a sign of victory also.

Down the road, there is still more He will bring us through. Our plan is not His plan but His plan is better. We might get wet, but we won't drown. We might get hot, but we won't burn. God is at work in our rain-soaking storms and coal hot fires, even when we can't see it. We can't see the wind but we know it's there. We can't see God, but we must believe He is there.

Learn to recognize and acknowledge God in the hard times and it will change the way you make decisions and ultimately change the outcome, no matter how hard the journey. "Trust in the Lord with all your heart, do not depend on your own understanding. Seek His will in all you do, and He will show you which path to take" (Prov. 3:5-6 NIV). "Commit your actions to the Lord, and your plans will succeed" (Prov. 16:3 NIV).

All these lessons and revelations are extremely valuable to me daily because I am human and must keep whatever I have learned in my heart to move forward. Jesus didn't come to earth to help us "get through" life. He didn't come to make us happy and make our lives go perfectly. He came to draw us and God closer together. We are separated because of our sin and we needed to be drawn back to God. We must conquer every barrier preventing us from a relationship with Him. So, apart from a transformation into becoming more like Him, we are not that "special" unless we have followed through with His Gospel, repented, been saved, and been baptized. We are "a chosen people". As a result, we can show others the goodness of God.

We live in a fallen world and life is not always good. Jesus told us, in the world we would have tribulation, but He has overcome it. The real cancer is the sin we will have in our lives. "The wages of sin is death," but He brings the gift of life! The only cure is a deep, unlimited, immeasurable relationship with God, with or without tribulations. Honor Him with your mind and body (1 Cor. 10:31), whether in joy or sorrow, victory or celebration, in life or death. Allow Him to transform you and use you for His glory. Make every day, month and year of your life greater and greater.

On that final day when we arrive in Heaven, He will look at us and say, My work is finished. We will be healed and be lustrous pearls. "The old has passed away and the new has come" (2 Cor. 5:17 NLT). No more physical or spiritual cancer. "But thank God! He gives us victory over sin and death through our Lord Jesus Christ. (2 Cor. 15:57) [NLT]

"Live deep in the oceans of life. Learn to take your eyes off the shoreline. I stayed up all night to see where the sun went. Then it dawned on me." Ingrid Simmonds

ABOUT
KHARIS PUBLISHING

KHARIS PUBLISHING is an independent, traditional publishing house with a core mission to publish impactful books, and channel proceeds into establishing mini-libraries or resource centers for orphanages in developing countries, so these kids will learn to read, dream, and grow. Every time you purchase a book from Kharis Publishing or partner as an author, you are helping give these kids an amazing opportunity to read, dream, and grow. Kharis Publishing is an imprint of Kharis Media LLC. Learn more at
https://www.kharispublishing.com.